Stress-Free Science

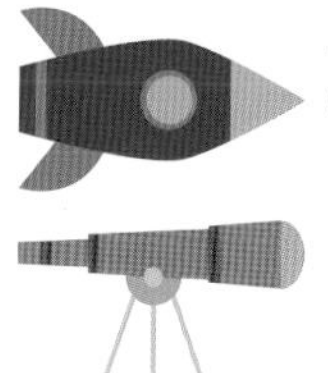

FEATURES Earth Sciences • Physical Sciences
Life Sciences • Space Sciences • Scientific Equipment

Stress-Free Science

A Visual Guide to Acing Science in Grades 4–8

Laurie E. Westphal, Ed.D.

Prufrock Press Inc.
Waco, Texas

Library of Congress Control Number:2019954824

Edited by Katy McDowall

Cover and layout design by Allegra Denbo

ISBN-13: 978-1-64632-016-5

Prufrock Press Inc.
P.O. Box 8813
Waco, TX 76714-8813
Phone: (800) 998-2208
Fax: (800) 240-0333
http://www.prufrock.com

Special thanks and lots of love to:
Ken and Irene Westphal, my mom and dad.

You have always been there for me, excluding the backyard swing incident, of course.

Table of Contents

Introduction

> Science is a way of thinking much more than it is a body of knowledge.
>
> —Carl Sagan

As Carl Sagan stated, the study of science is much more than just facts and knowledge; yet without the specialized vocabulary that accompanies the scientific concepts and processes, you may find yourself at a disadvantage as you strive to express yourself scientifically. That is where *Stress-Free Science* comes to the rescue.

This visual guide is much more than a list of words and definitions. The vocabulary used in science is vast. Many of the words resemble commonly used words; however, their scientific usage may be very different. There also are many science words that are new and difficult for students to remember. These are the terms found in this guide—those new and seemingly difficult words or those that have significantly different definitions than common language. You will also find common examples, graphics, and illustrations to build your understanding.

This book also addresses other information that will help you on your way to becoming a scientific thinker. You will find diagrams and graphics of the different cycles studied in the science classroom. There also is a reference guide devoted to commonly used formulas and units used in science. This book has an entire section devoted to the equipment and glassware that you may work with in the science classroom, including a definition and visual (for easy identification) and if appropriate, specific directions for the equipment's use—such as how to transport liquid in an eyedropper without blowing air into the liquid and turning it upside down.

In addition to equipment, there also is a quick reference section to assist you with the various steps of the scientific method, from creating testable questions to writing procedures and how to visibly present data through the creation of different types of graphs. You can quickly flip to the instructions on multiple line graphs and be on your way to producing your own. These quick reference pages are meant to assist you in the steps of the scientific method in a quick, concise way.

Once you use a reference like this book, you'll agree that it truly is absolutely essential. It will be the reference material you will use again and again to supplement and reinforce topics throughout your science classes.

Visual Definitions by Topic

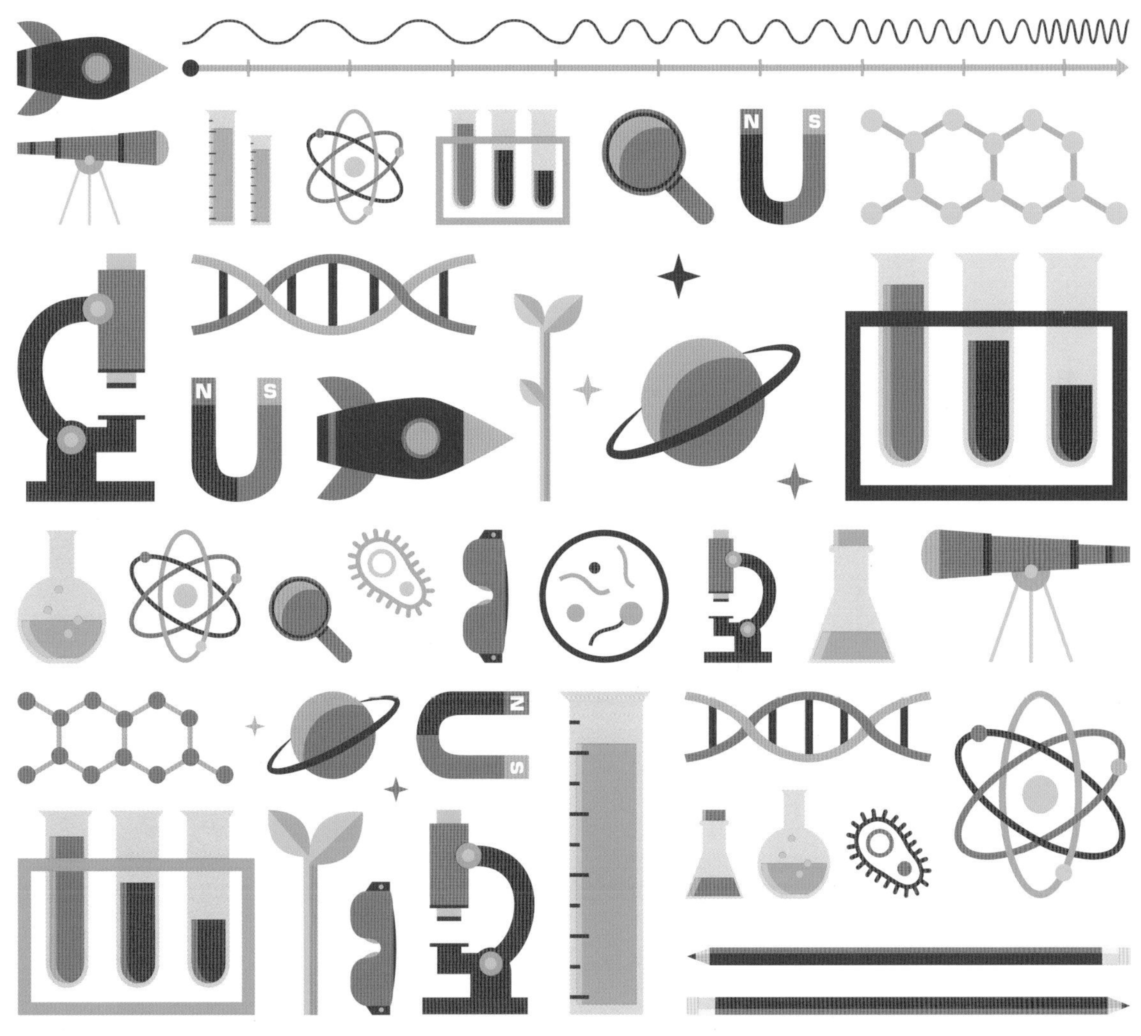

SCIENTIFIC EQUIPMENT

Anemometer

A weather instrument used to measure wind force and speed.

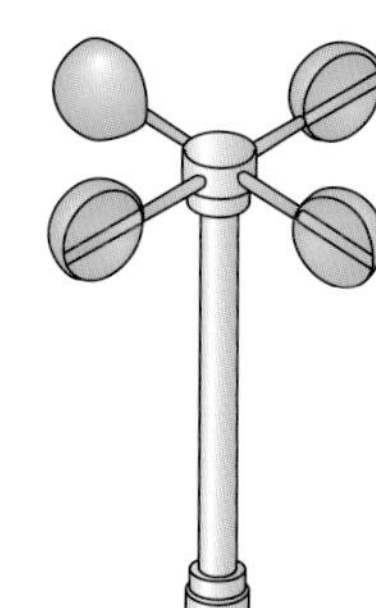

Barometer

A weather instrument used to measure atmospheric pressure. Below 29 is considered rainy or stormy, while 30 or above is considered fair weather.

Beaker

A container used to transport, pour, or mix liquids. It cannot measure an exact amount of liquid.

Bunsen Burner

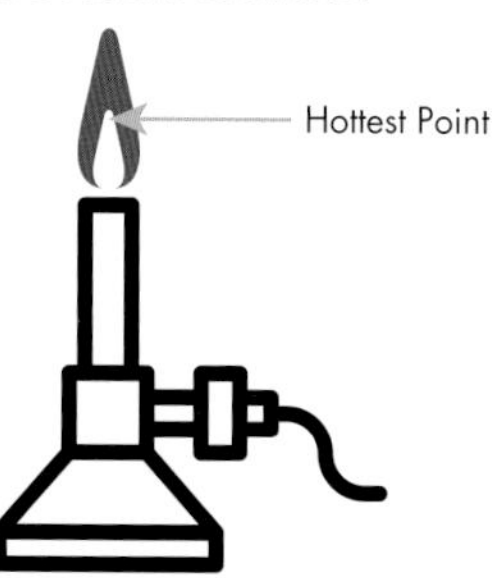

A small burner used in the laboratory. It is connected to a gas source and uses a very hot flame. When heating, the hottest area is at the top of the inner core.

Compass

An instrument used to find direction. It usually is made of a magnetic needle that is free to move until it is lined up with Earth's magnetic field.

CO–FU

Compound Light Microscope

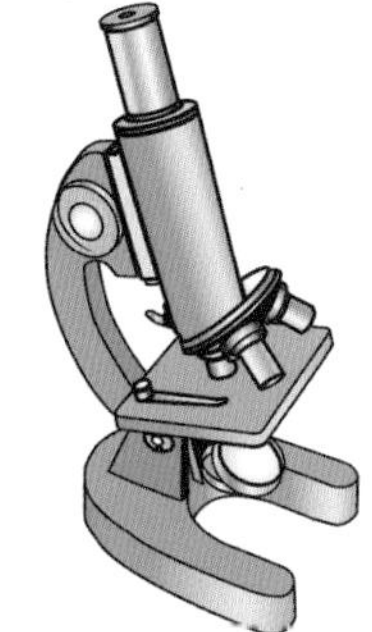

A light microscope that has more than one lens that is used to magnify a small object or specimen. See page 111 for instructions for using a microscope.

Erlenmeyer Flask

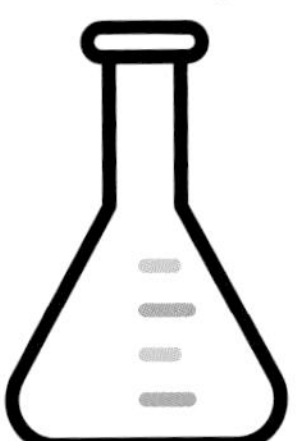

A flat-bottomed, cone-shaped flask used for mixing and heating liquids. A stopper can be used to seal it.

Eyedropper

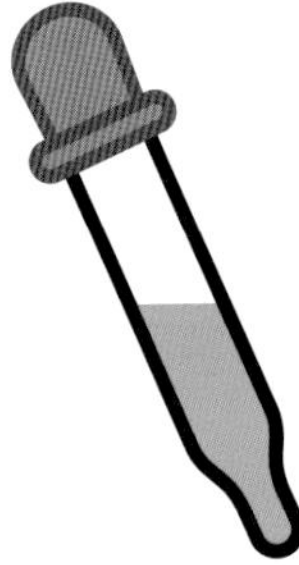

A tube with a rubber bulb on the end that is used to pull liquid into the tube. It is used for transporting small amounts of liquid. See page 114 for instructions for using an eyedropper.

Eyewash

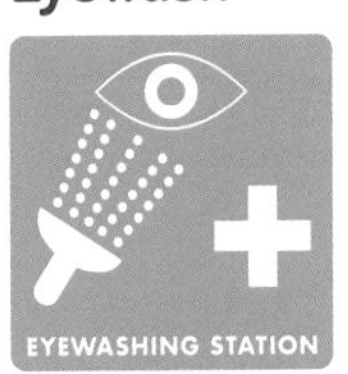

Safety equipment that is used to flush or wash the eyes in case something gets into them during a lab experiment.

Fire Blanket

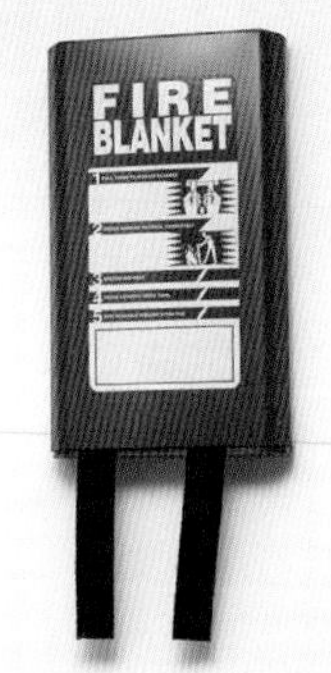

A blanket that be used to put out a small fire or wrap around someone in case of fire. They are usually stored in red bags or boxes.

Funnel

A utensil used to pour small solids or liquids into small-mouthed containers. It is usually made of either plastic or glass.

Goggles

Safety equipment used to protect your eyes during an experiment. Some goggles just protect your eyes from projectiles; others also protect against gasses that might be created during an experiment.

Graduated Cylinder

A cylinder that has been marked with different "graduations," or lines and numbers, to show the level of the liquid put in it. Always read the meniscus (see p. 8), or the bottom of the curved liquid, when using a glass graduated cylinder. See page 114 for instructions for reading a graduated cylinder.

Hand Lens

A handheld magnifying glass that allows you to look closely at objects. The typical magnification is 10x; it makes the object you are examining 10 times bigger.

Hot Plate

A device used to heat beakers or flasks. It either has coils or a ceramic plate for heating. Always be sure the cord is tucked away for safety!

Hydrion Paper

A special kind of litmus paper that turns different colors depending on the pH (acidity or alkalinity) of the substance being tested. Once the substance is tested, you compare the color of the paper to the color on the container to determine the pH.

Litmus Paper

Paper used to determine pH. The paper changes color depending on whether it has been put in an acid, base, or neutral substance. Red litmus paper will turn blue when placed in a base, and blue litmus paper will turn red when placed in an acid.

Meniscus

The lowest part of the curve created by water when it is placed in a glass graduated cylinder. When reading the exact amount in a glass graduated cylinder, you look at where the meniscus lies.

Meter Stick

A common instrument for measuring length in the classroom. It is broken down into centimeters, the large numbers on the meterstick (100 cm = 1 m), and millimeters, the small lines (1,000 mm = 1 m).

Pan Balance

A balance that uses two different pans to find the mass of an object. See page 113 for instructions for using a pan balance.

Petri Dish

A shallow dish approximately 10 centimeters in diameter, used for growing bacteria cultures or evaporating crystals.

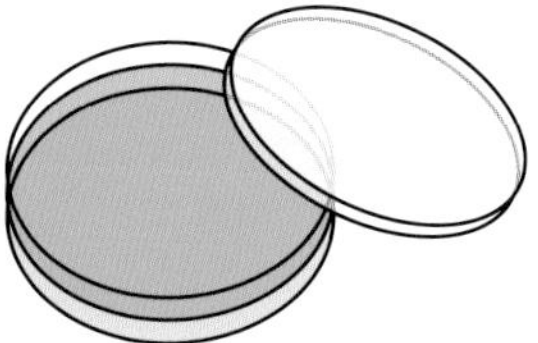

Ring Stand

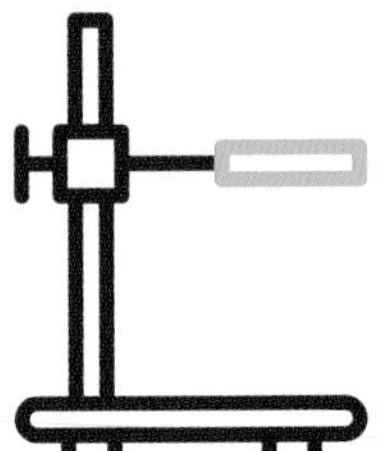

A metal stand that usually includes a ring and is used to support glassware during heating or other lab equipment during an experiment.

Spring Scale

A measuring device or scale that uses a spring to measure the weight of an object. The most common unit measured using a spring scale is Newtons; 4.45 Newtons equals 1 pound. See page 113 for instructions for using a spring scale.

Stirring Rod

Stirring rods are usually made of glass and are used for mixing chemicals and liquids.

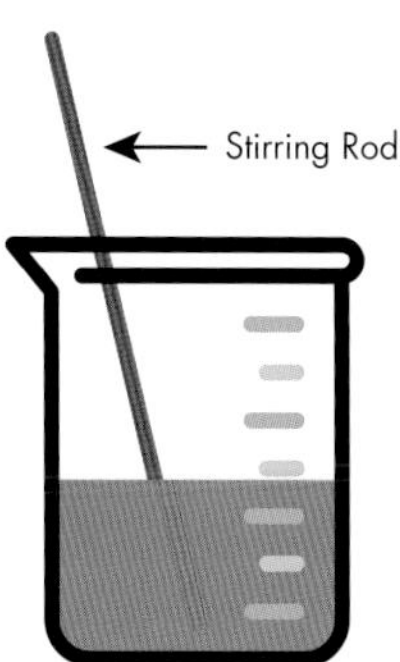

Stopper

A cork or plug that is placed in glassware to seal it. It can be made of cork, plastic, or rubber, and can either be solid or have holes in it to allow glass tubing to pass through.

Stream Table

A long table that is used to show weathering, erosion, and water flow in streams and bodies of water.

Telescope

An instrument that uses lenses and mirrors to view faraway objects. There are three types: reflecting, refracting, and radio, which does not have any lenses or mirrors but depends on radio waves given off by faraway objects in space.

Reflecting

Refracting

Radio

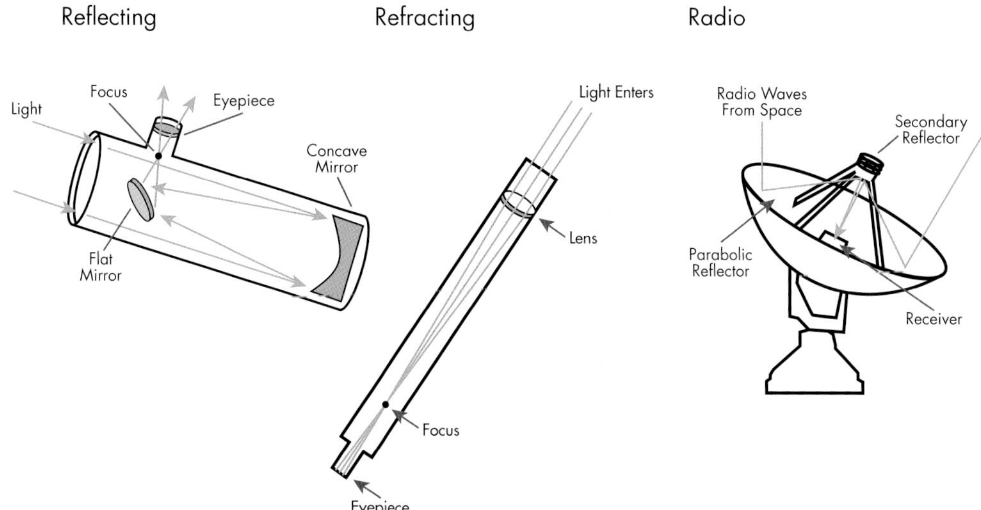

TE–TR

Test Tube

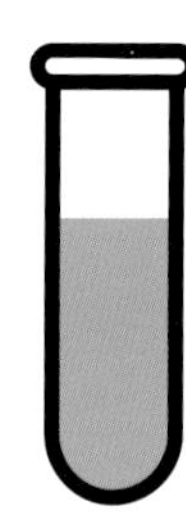

A long glass tube that has one end open with the other end rounded. It can be used for heating, mixing, or collecting chemicals. Because it has a rounded bottom and cannot stand on its own, it usually needs to be kept in a rack.

Test Tube Brush

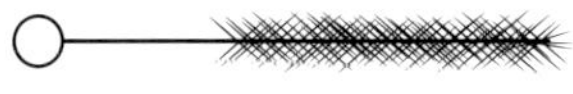

A long-handled brush used for cleaning test tubes.

Test Tube Clamp

A clamp designed specifically to hold test tubes while they are being heated. To open the clamp, squeeze the middle loops.

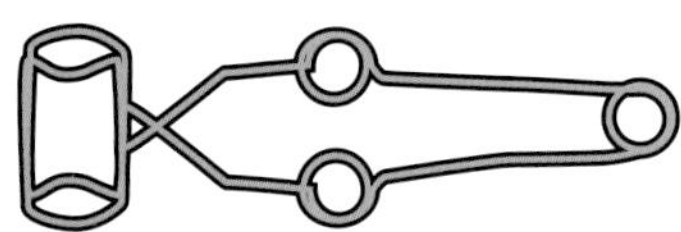

Test Tube Rack

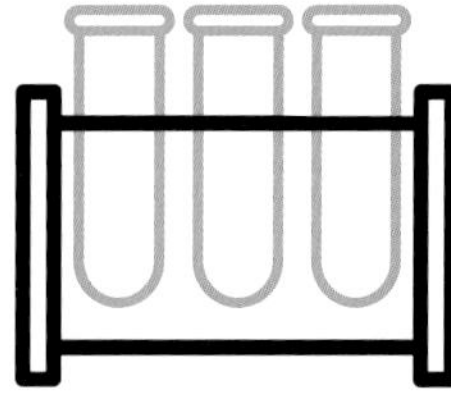

A rack made of wood or plastic specifically designed to hold test tubes while they are being used. Some also have a row of rods in the back on which to place the test tubes upside down for drying.

Thermometer

A device used to measure temperature. It contains mercury or colored alcohol, which expands and rises in the thermometer as the temperature increases. Thermometers measure temperatures in Celsius or Fahrenheit, or both. Some current thermometers provide digital readings.

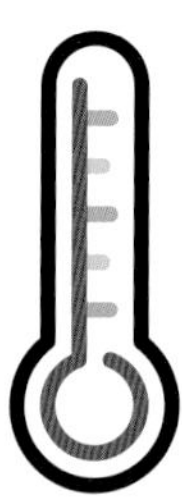

Triple Beam Balance

A balance that is used to determine the mass of an object. See page 112 for instructions for using a triple beam balance.

THE SCIENTIFIC PROCESS

Accuracy

A measurement that is close to an intended measurement or value. For example, when shooting at a target, marks are considered accurate when they are close to the bullseye.

Bar Graph

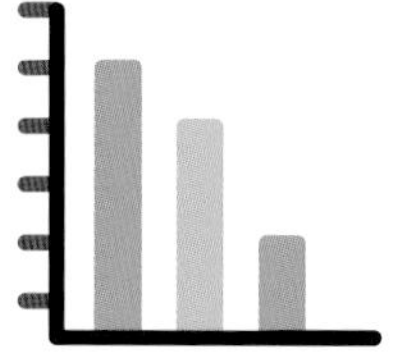

A graph or chart that shows information using bars. It should be used to compare qualities of data. See pages 120–121 for more information about creating a bar graph.

Circle Graph

A graph that shows results in a proportional manner or compares relative sizes of outcomes in an experiment.

Conclusion

A summarization of the results of the experiment and their impact on the hypothesis.

"In this activity, my hypothesis was not correct. I . . ."

Control (Controlled Variables)

All of the aspects of an experiment that are kept constant and not changed. In a well-planned experiment, all of the factors should be controlled except the independent (manipulated) variable.

Example:
When testing how the height of a ramp affects the time it takes a car to go down it, the following are controlled: same ramp, same car, same timer, same person who takes the time, and same release technique of the car.

Control (Control Group)

When designing an experiment, this group or object remains as it is; no changes are made to it.

Example:
When testing how the amount of water affects the growth of a plant, the constants might include type of pot, type and size of plant, amount of soil, amount and frequency of fertilizer, and amount of sunlight.

Data

A group of facts or measurements gathered either through research or experimentation.

Data Table

A table that is designed to record quantitative information gained in an experiment.

The Effect of Ramp Height on Car's Travel Time				
Height of ramp (cm)	Time of Car on Track (sec)			Average of the trials
	Trial 1	Trial 2	Trial 3	
5 cm	6.4 sec	6.2 sec	6.9 sec	6.5 sec
10 cm	5.2 sec	5.0 sec	4.8 sec	5.0 sec
15 cm	3.2 sec	3.5 sec	3.3 sec	3.3 sec

Dependent Variable

The outcome or results of the experiment; another name for the responding variable. Recorded on the vertical or y-axis when creating line graphs.

Example:
When testing the effect of a heat lamp on the evaporation of water in a graduated cylinder, the amount of water left in the cylinder is the dependent variable.

Dependent Variable, continued

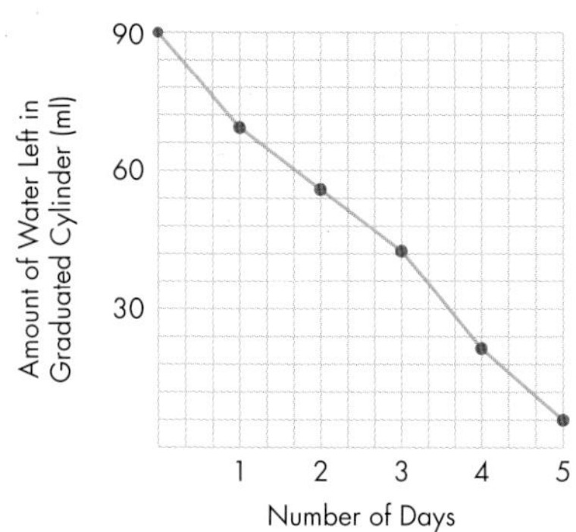

Hypothesis

An educated guess or prediction (based on either research or previous experience) about the result of an experiment.

Examples:
If a ramp is raised higher, it will take less time for a car to travel down it. Based on previous experiments, the bigger the wheels on the car, the faster it will travel.

Independent Variable

The variable that is changed in an experiment; another name for a manipulated variable.

Example:
When testing the effect of a heat lamp on the evaporation of water in a graduated cylinder, the number of days is the independent variable.

Inference

Using an observation to develop a conclusion.

Example:
In the picture, we can observe a broken window and a baseball on the floor. Based on the observations, we could make an *inference* that the baseball broke the window.

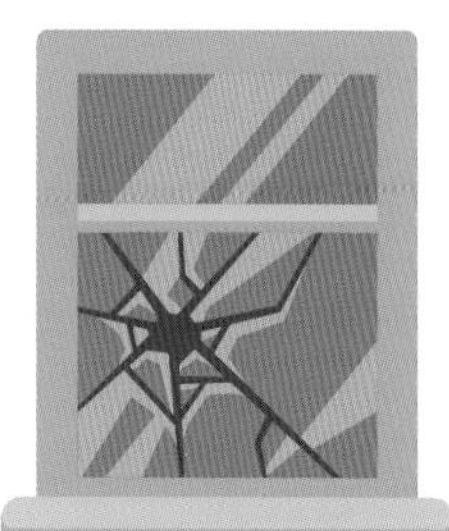

Law

A statement based on something observed in the world around us.

Example:
The Universal Law of Gravitation explains why all objects fall at the same rate on Earth.

Line Graph

A graph that shows information using lines; usually used to show data that were collected over time.

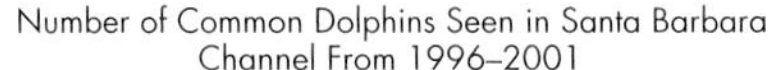

Number of Common Dolphins Seen in Santa Barbara
Channel From 1996–2001

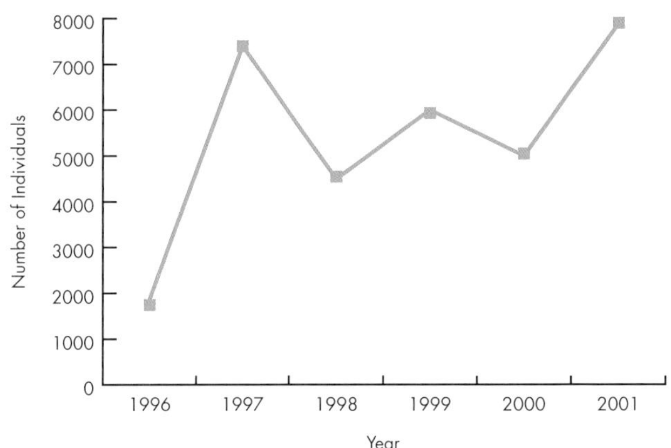

Line of Best Fit

A line that shows the average of the data shown on a scatterplot. This line is often used when extrapolating or predicting information using the data collected from an experiment.

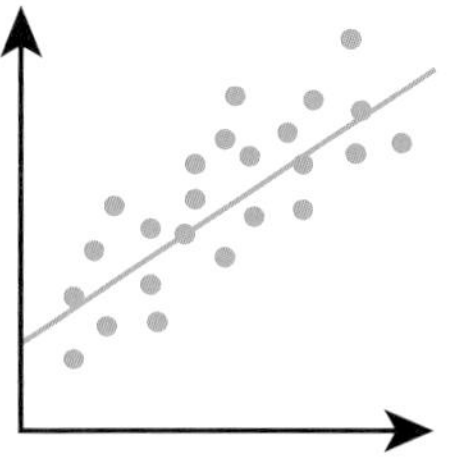

Manipulated Variable

The variable that is changed in an experiment; another name for an independent variable.

Observation

The act of gathering data by using one or more of the five senses. (*Note*: You should never smell, taste, or touch anything during a science experiment.)

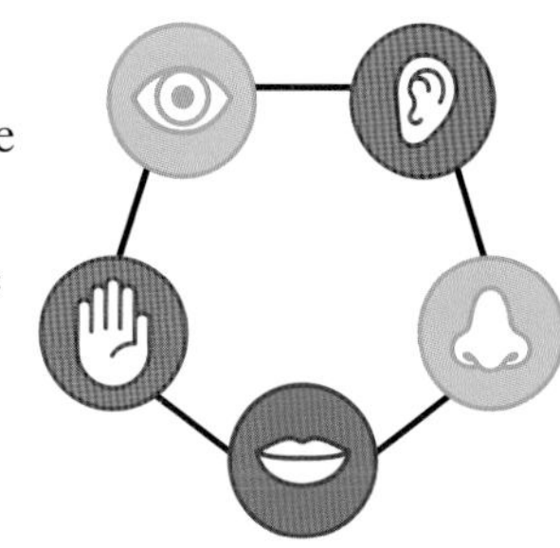

Precision

The closeness of two or more measures to each other.

Example:
When shooting at a target, marks are precise if they are close together. *Note*: In this drawing, although precise, the marks are not accurate because they are not near the center of the target.

Problem/Testable Question

The question to be considered and addressed in an experiment. The hypothesis usually answers this question.

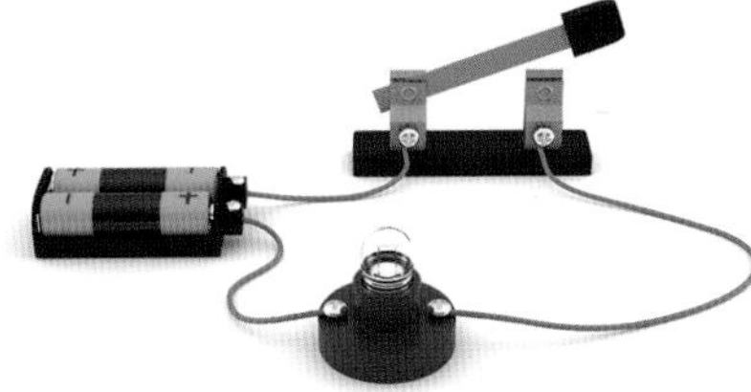

Examples:
How does the number of batteries affect the strength of the current in a circuit?
Does water temperature affect the breathing rate of goldfish?

Procedure

The steps or plans that need to be followed to complete an experiment.

Qualitative Data/Observation

Characteristic or quality that describes what is being observed; based on a person's opinion. Do not involve numbers or measurements.

Examples:
Color, texture, taste, likes or dislikes, comparisons (e.g., Stan is taller than me.)

Quantitative Data/Observation

Observation that can be measured and recorded using quantities or numbers.

Examples:
Mass, length, volume, number of something, recorded time

Responding Variable

The outcome of the experiment; another name for the dependent variable. This variable is recorded on the vertical or y-axis when creating line graphs.

Example:
When testing the effect of a heat lamp on the evaporation of water in a graduated cylinder, the amount of water left in the cylinder is the dependent variable.

Scatterplot

A graph created by plotting multiple data points. The purpose of this graph is to see how one variable affects another. The correlation (or relationship) can be positive, negative, or none (no correlation).

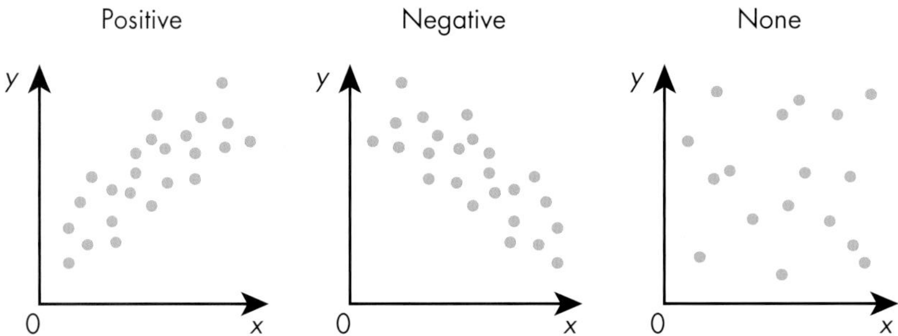

Scientific Method

A tool used by scientists to find the answer to a question or problem. The steps of the scientific method are:

1. Identify the problem.
2. Conduct research.
3. Create a hypothesis.

Scientific Method, continued

4. Perform an experiment.
5. Analyze the data.
6. Develop a conclusion.

Theory

A general principle or idea that explains facts or past events or that can be used to predict future events.

Trial

A test that is conducted more than once during an experiment.

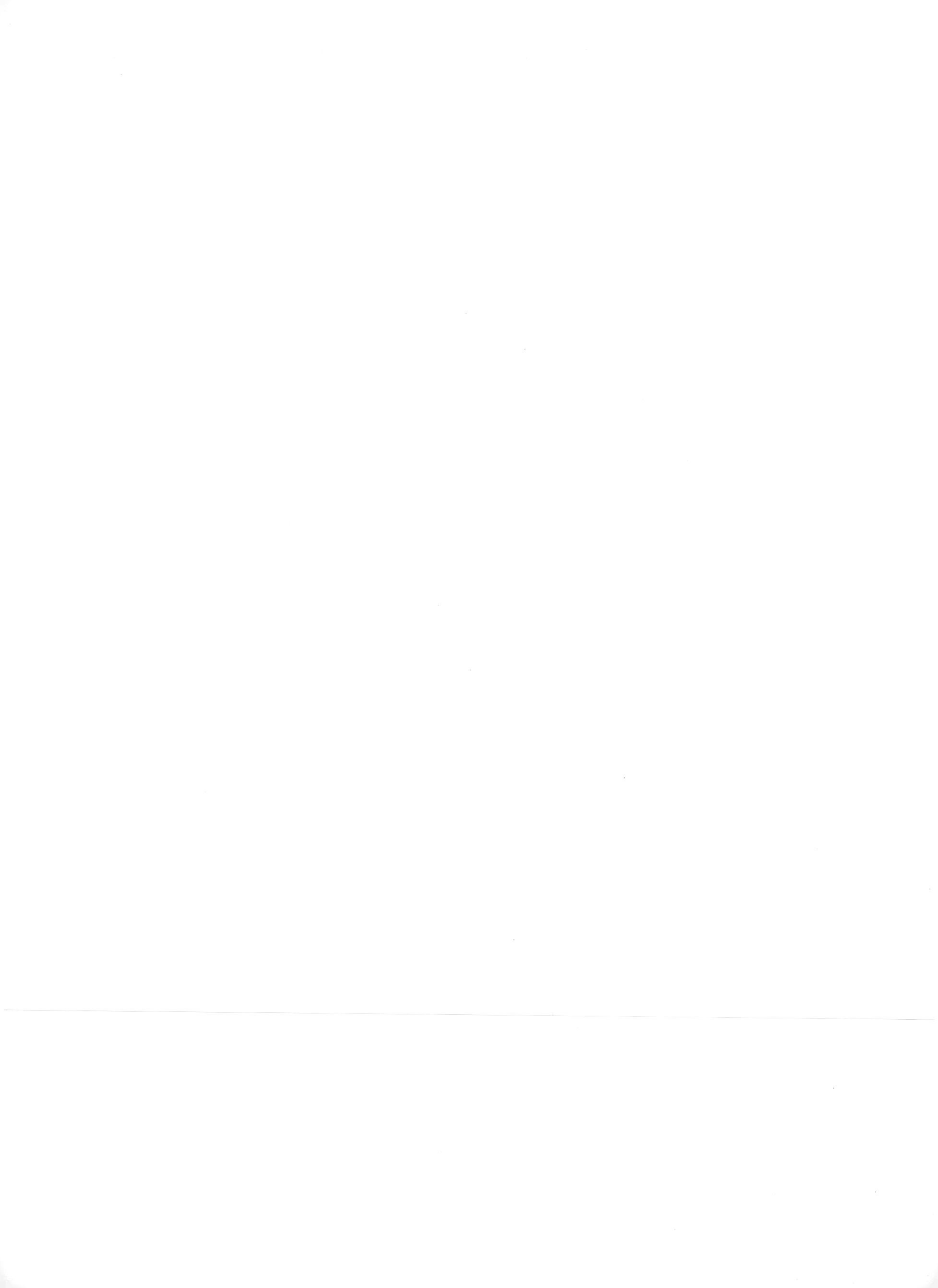

MEASUREMENTS AND UNITS

Ampere (A)

The unit for electric current or the number of electrons passing a point in a certain amount of time.

Astronomical Unit (AU)

The unit used to measure long distances in space. It is equal to the distance from the Earth to the sun.

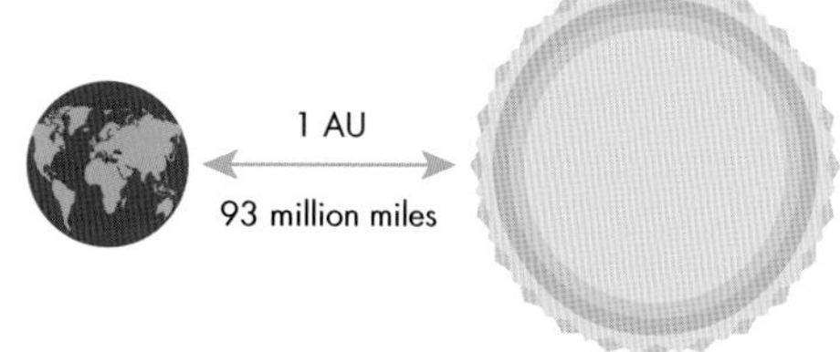

1 AU = 149,597,870,691 km (149.60×10^9 m)
1 AU = 93 million miles (9.3×10^7 mi)

Calorie (cal)

A unit of energy; kilocalories (1,000 calories) are commonly used to describe the amount of energy found in food.

1,000 calories = 1 kilocalorie
1 calorie = 4.18 joules

Celsius (°C)

The metric temperature scale on which water freezes at 0° and boils at 100°.

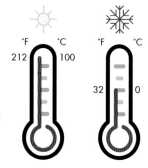

Fahrenheit (°F)

The standard temperature scale at which water freezes at 32° and boils at 212°.

Gram (g)

The basic metric unit used to measure mass.

1 gram = 1,000 milligrams
1,000 grams = 1 kilogram

Gravity Constant (g_c)

The speed at which an object will accelerate as it falls toward Earth (until it reaches terminal velocity). It is also called the acceleration due to gravity.

$g_c = 9.8$ m/sec^2

Hertz (Hz)

The metric unit for frequency. It is the number of waves that pass a certain point in one second.

1 Hertz = 1 wave/second

Joule (J)

The metric unit for energy and heat.

1 joule = 1 Newton of force • 1 meter
1 joule = 1 watt/1 second
4.18 joules = 1 calorie

Kelvin (°K)

The temperature scale that begins at absolute zero, where there is no molecular movement. Water freezes at 273 °K and boils at 373 °K.

°Kelvin = °Celsius + 273

Light Year (ly)

The amount of distance light can travel through space in one year. It is used to measure long distances in space. A light year equals about 9.461 trillion (9.461×10^{12}) kilometers or 5.879 (5.879×10^{12}) trillion miles.

Example:
Our nearest star is 4.4 light years away, so it takes light from that star 4.4 years to reach the Earth.

Liter (l)

A metric unit for volume.

1,000 liters = 1 cubic meter (m^3)
1 liter = 1,000 milliliters
1,000 liters = 1 kiloliter

Meter (m)

The basic metric unit of length.

1 meter = 1,000 millimeters
1 meter = 100 centimeters
1,000 meters = 1 kilometer

Newton (N)

The metric unit for force. It is equal to the amount of force needed to accelerate a mass of one kilogram at a rate of one meter per second per second.

1 Newton = 1 kg • m/s^2
4.45 Newtons = 1 pound

Ohm (Ω)

The metric unit for resistance.

1 ohm = 1 volt/1 ampere

Pascal

The standard metric unit for pressure.

1 pascal = 1 Newton/meter
101,325 pascal = 1 atmosphere

Volt (V)

The standard metric unit for voltage or the force of electricity.

1 volt = 1 ohm • 1 ampere

Watts (W)

The standard metric unit for power. It is equal to one joule of energy per second.

1 watt = 1 joule/1 sec
1,000 watts = 1 kilowatt
1,000,000 watts = 1 megawatt

LIFE SCIENCES

Abiotic

Factors that are not biological (or living).

Examples:
Temperature, weather, landforms

Acquired Traits

Abilities that are helpful to an organism but are not passed on from a parent.

Example:
Large arm muscles developed by training for a sporting event

Allele

A genetic trait and a member of a pair of genes on a chromosome. Represented by a letter, written in pairs, and used in Punnett squares to predict possible outcomes of a genetic cross.

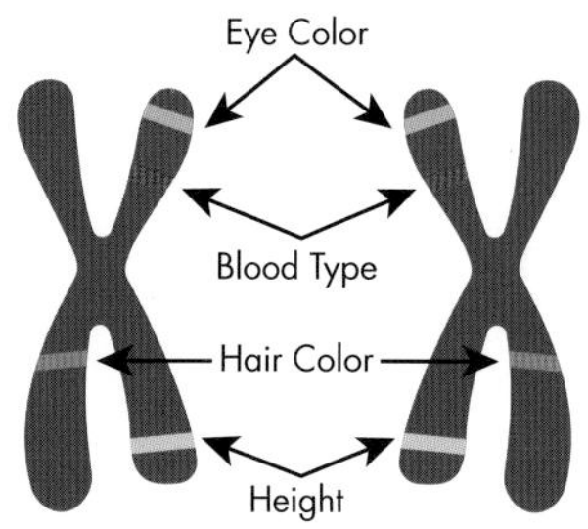

Amphibian

A cold-blooded vertebrate that is born underwater, using its gills to breathe, and then spends the rest of its life on land, using lungs to breathe.

Examples:
Frogs, salamanders, toads, newts

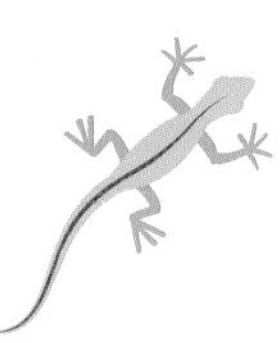

Anaphase

The stage of mitosis and meiosis when the chromosomes are separated from each other.

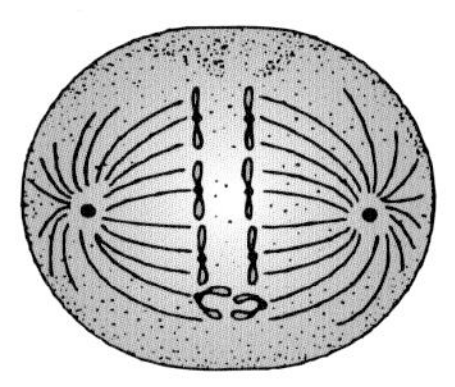

Anther

The part of the flower that produces and contains the pollen.

Arachnid

An arthropod that has mandibles (a special kind of jaw), eight appendages (legs), and a cephalothorax (connected head and thorax).

Examples:
Spiders, ticks, scorpions

Archaebacteria

Considered "ancient" bacteria. There are three main types that live in extreme conditions: thermoacidophile (extreme heat or acid), halophile (high salt), and methanogens (produce methane).

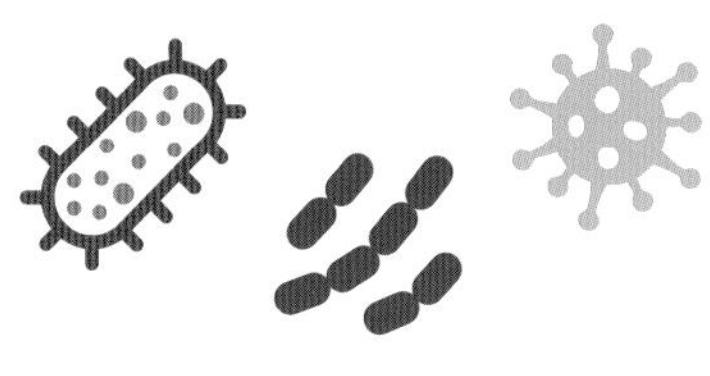

Arthropod

Animals that have segmented bodies, jointed exoskeletons, and bilateral symmetry (looks the same on the right and left side).

Examples:
Insects, spiders, crabs, scorpions, centipedes

Autotroph

A living thing that can make its own food, usually through photosynthesis.

Examples:
Plants, blue-green algae

Binary Fission

When an organism reproduces by copying its genetic material and then dividing into two parts that are the same.

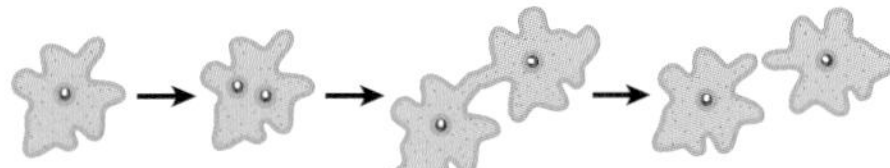

Biodiversity

The variety of living things within a biome or ecosystem.

Biome

A large geographical area of the Earth's surface that has a certain set of characteristics.

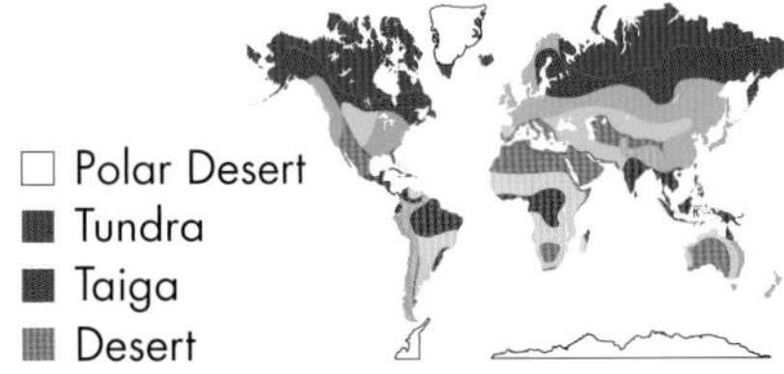

Examples:
Tundra, taiga, grassland, fresh water, saltwater, deciduous forest, desert, tropical rain forest

Biotic

Factors that are biological (or living).

Examples:
Producers, consumers, decomposers

Camouflage

An adaptation that helps an animal blend into its surrounding and helps it avoid predators.

Example:
The arctic fox has white fur in the winter and brown fur in the summer.

Carbon (Dioxide) Cycle

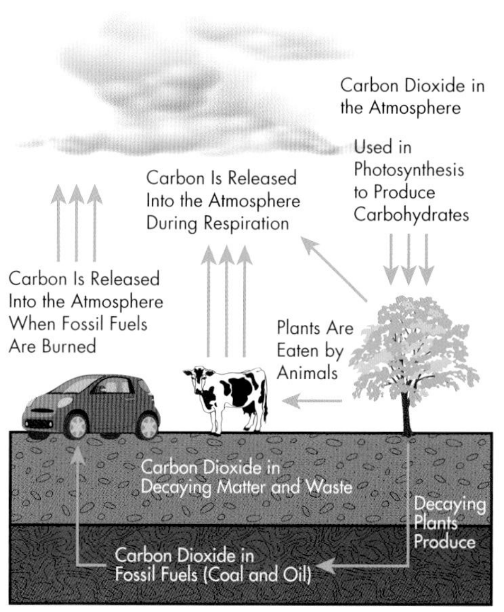

The way in which carbon (in the form of carbon dioxide) is removed from the atmosphere by living things and ultimately returned to the atmosphere.

Carnivore

Any living thing with a diet consisting mostly of meat.

Examples:
Lions, Venus flytraps, bears

Carrying Capacity

The amount of living things a biome or ecosystem can "carry" or sustain based on the number of resources found within it. See page 37.

Cell

The smallest functional unit of all living things.

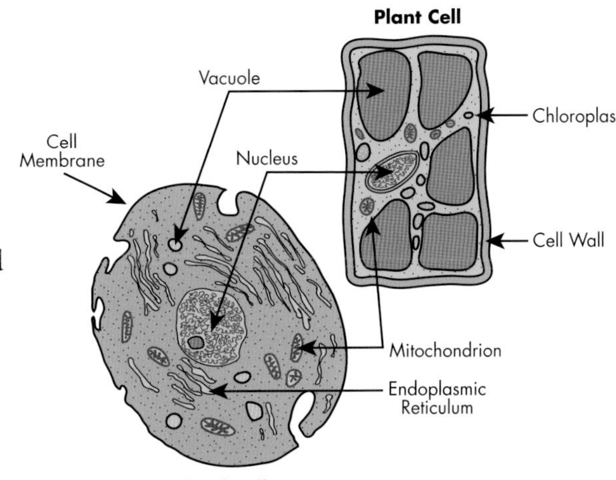

Cell Membrane

The barrier around a cell's cytoplasm (see cell).

Cell Theory

Accepted belief about cells. The theory includes the belief that all living organisms are made of cells, cells are the basic unit for all structures in living things, and all cells come from other cells.

Cell Wall

Rigid protective outer wall around a plant cell.

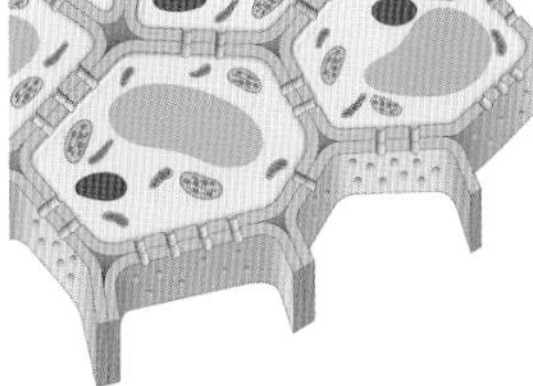

Chloroplast

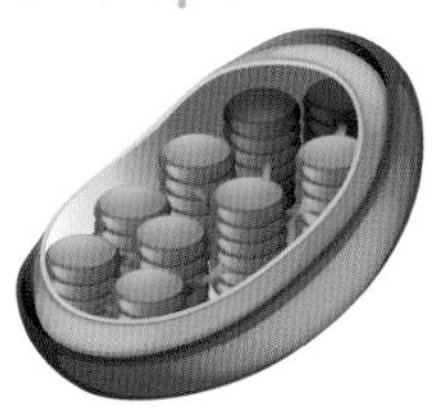

Organelle filled with chlorophyll in a plant where photosynthesis takes place.

Chordate

Animals with notochords (central nervous system on their backs).

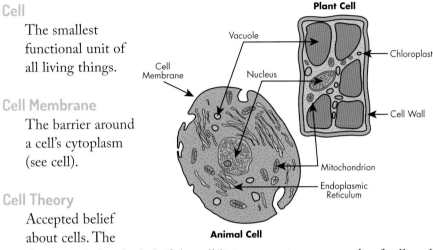

Examples:
Vertebrates, sea squirts, and lancelets

Classification

The processes scientists use to group and identify living things.

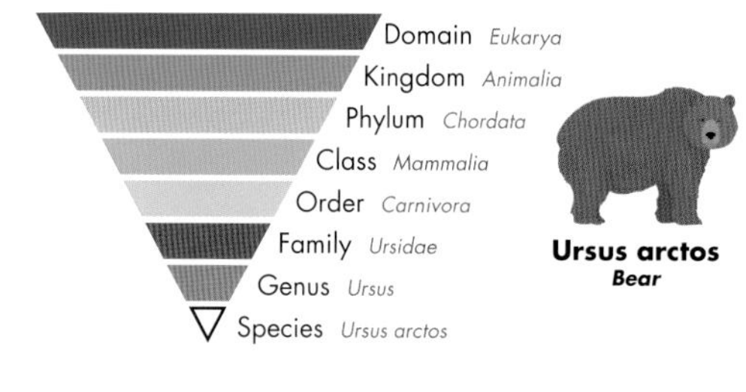

Climate

Weather conditions in an area for a long period time that define biotic and abiotic aspects in that area.

Examples:
Tropical, polar, temperate, equatorial

Codominance

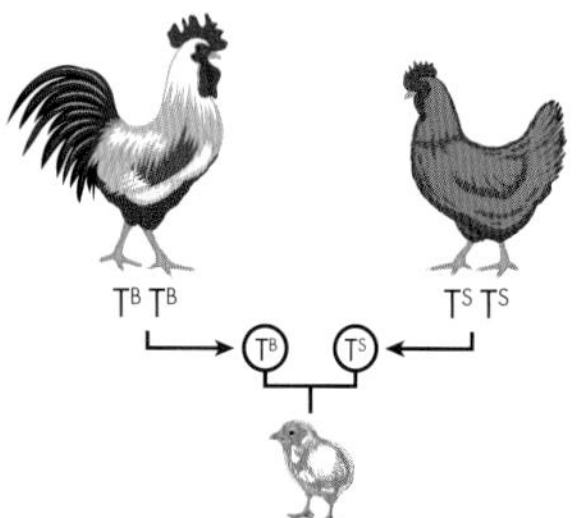

In genetics, a relationship in which neither allele is dominant.

Example:
A white and brown chicken are bred, and the offspring have spots and are both white and brown.

Cold-Blooded

A living thing that cannot control its body temperature. Its temperature is determined by its environment.

Example:
In order to get warm, a lizard or snake will lie on warm sand or in direct sunlight to bring up its body temperature.

Commensalism

A symbiotic relationship between organisms in which one of them benefits from the relationship and the other is not affected.

Examples:
Barnacles that attach themselves to whales (and ships) or spiders that use trees to create and support their webs

Consumer

An organism that feeds on plants or other animals.

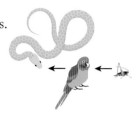

Cytoplasm

The jelly-like material inside a cell.

Deciduous Forest

Biomes in which the trees lose their leaves each year.

Decomposer

An organism that breaks down dead animals and decaying matter into other substances.

Examples:
Bacteria, fungi

Desert

An ecosystem that has low levels of rainfall. Deserts can be cold.

Examples:
Sahara, Gobi, Mojave, Antarctica

Dichotomous Key

A key that allows you to identify an item based on a series of choices.

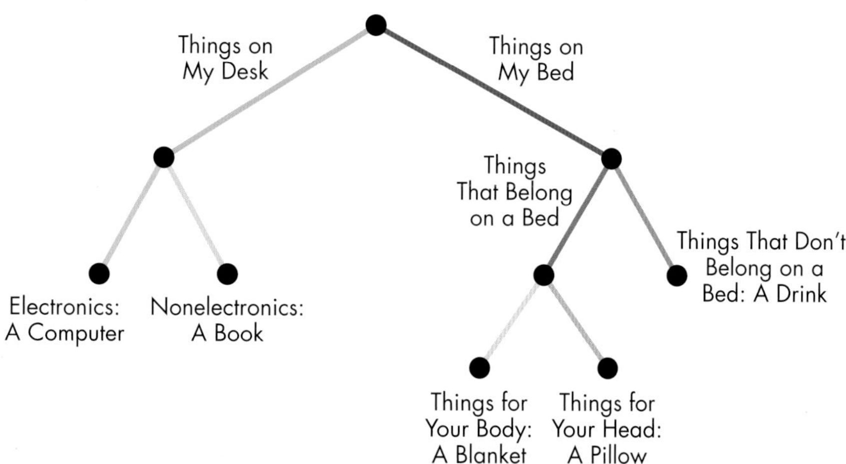

DNA (Deoxyribonucleic Acid)

The molecule that carries the genetic information in a cell. It has a "twisted ladder" or double helix shape.

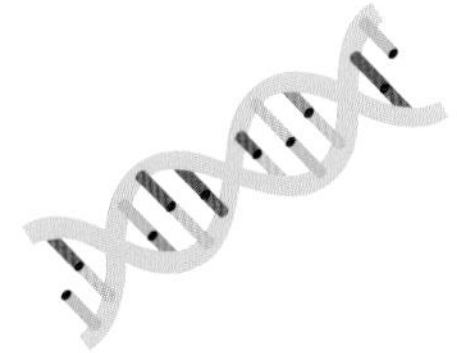

Dominant Trait

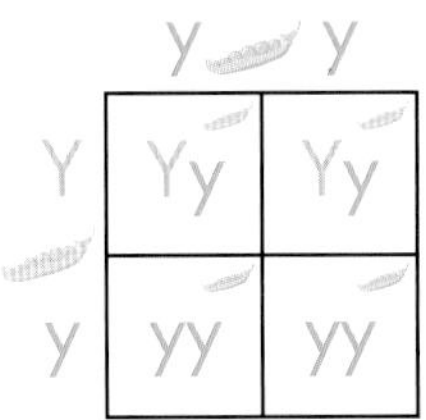

A trait that will appear in children (offspring) if one of the parents has the trait. It is written with a capital letter when writing the alleles for the traits in a Punnett square.

Example:
Because yellow is a dominant trait in pea plants, the yellow trait would be written as Y.

Note: Image adapted from "Punnett Square," by Pbrocks13, 2008, https://en.wikipedia.org/wiki/Punnett_square#/media/File:Punnett_Square.svg. CC BY-SA 3.0.

Endoplasmic Reticulum

A group of pathways in the cytoplasm of the cell that help move materials through the cell.

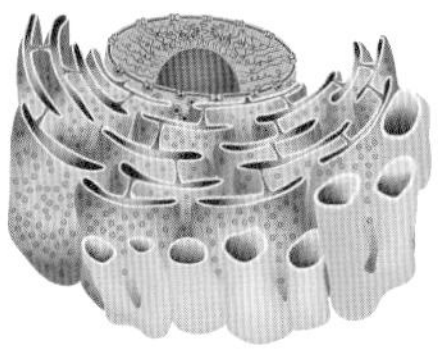

Energy Pyramid

A model that shows how energy flows in a community. Each level of the pyramid represents organisms in the food chain. The bottom of the pyramid is producers, who bring energy into the pyramid. Each level of the pyramid only gets 10% of the energy of the level below it.

Tertiary Consumers
Secondary Consumers
Primary Consumers
Primary Producers

Epidermis

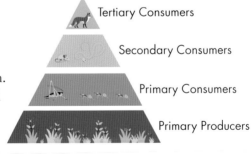

The outermost layer of the skin, or the outermost layer of a leaf.

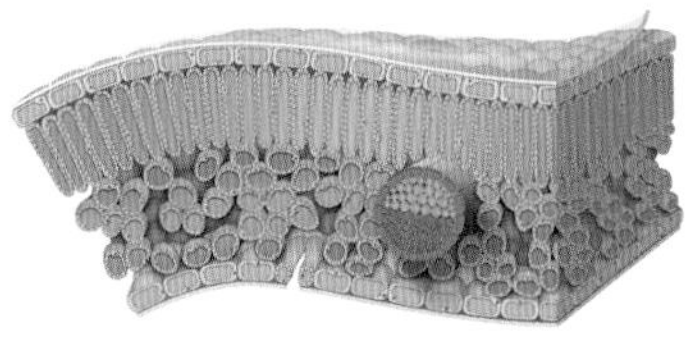

Eukaryote

An organism with genetic material (DNA) contained within a nucleus.

Examples:
Animal cells, plant cells

Extinct

A species that is no longer in existence.

Examples:
Tyrannosaurus rex, Dodo bird, Glyptodon

Filament

The long tube-like structure that holds up the anther of a plant.

Food Chain

The sequence of how living things eat each other in a biological community. It always starts with a primary energy source (usually the sun).

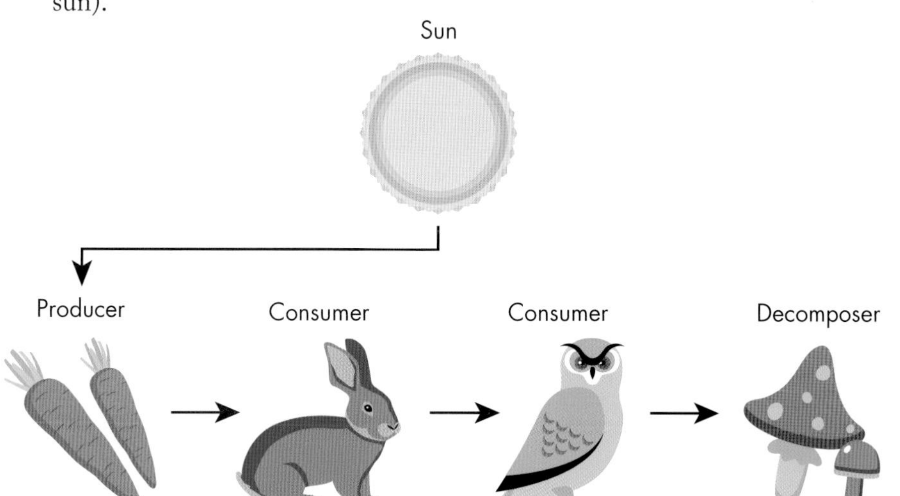

Food Web

Two or more food chains interconnected together.

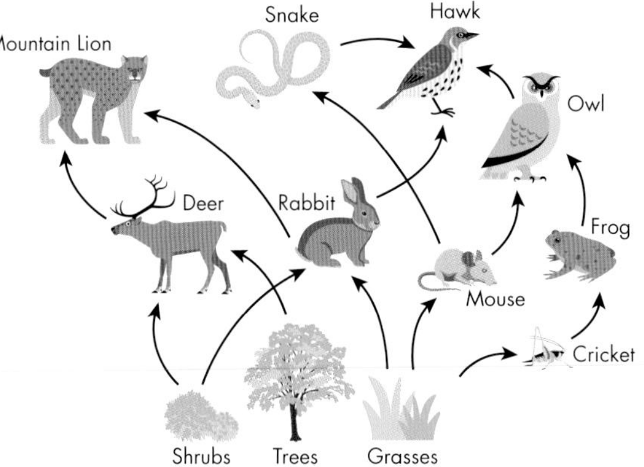

Fruit

The fleshy part of a plant that contains the seeds.

Examples:
Tomato, apple, orange

Fungi

Multicellular organisms that are best known for their decomposing role in most food webs.

Examples:
Yeast, mushrooms, truffles

Gene

In genetics, a unit of heredity that can be transferred from parent to offspring. Represented by a letter or allele.

Genotype

The genetic makeup of an organism as shown by the alleles or letters that represent the trait.

Example:
The genotype for a heterozygous purple pea plant would be: Pp.

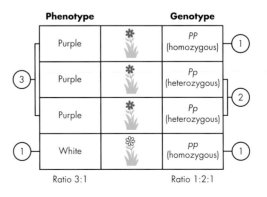

	Phenotype		Genotype	
3	Purple		*PP* (homozygous)	1
	Purple		*Pp* (heterozygous)	2
	Purple		*Pp* (heterozygous)	
1	White		*pp* (homozygous)	1
	Ratio 3:1		Ratio 1:2:1	

Genotypic Ratio

The ratio of the genotypes of predicted offspring using a Punnett square.

Example:
By using a Punnett square, you can calculate that the four possible offspring would be: PP, Pp, Pp, and pp. The genotypic ratio for this would be 1:2:1.

Genus

A category in the classification system. It is between species and family.

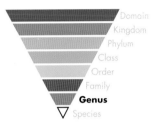

Domain
Kingdom
Phylum
Class
Order
Family
Genus
Species

Golgi Apparatus

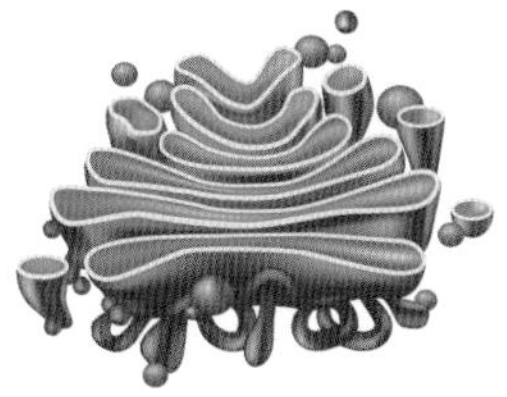

An organelle found in the cytoplasm of cells that processes and packages substances the cell needs.

Grassland/Savanna

A large area or ecosystem where most of the plants are grasses.

Habitat

The area or environment where an organism normally lives or has its needs met.

Herbivore

An organism that depends on plants for most of its food and energy.

Heterotroph

An organism that depends on other organisms as its food source.

Heterozygous

When an organism has two different alleles for a genetic trait.

Examples:
Pp is a heterozygous purple plant.

Hibernation

A state of inactivity in which an organism conserves energy through the colder months.

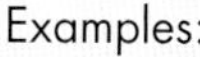

Examples:
Animals that hibernate include bats, bears, frogs, and hedgehogs.

Homeostasis

The ability of an organism to regulate itself in response to its environment.

Examples:
Shivering or sweating

Homologous Structures

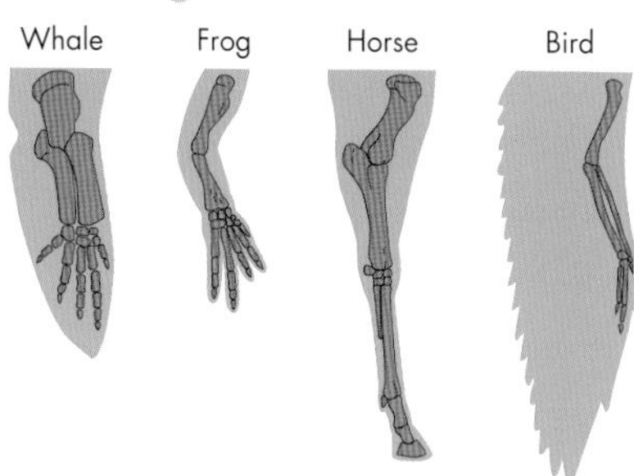

Similar structures that unrelated organisms share.

Examples:
Whale fin, frog leg, horse leg, bird wing

Homozygous

When an organism has two of the same alleles for a genetic trait.

Examples:
PP is a homozygous pink plant, or pp would be a homozygous white plant.

Hybrid

Another term for having heterozygous alleles for a certain trait.

Example:
Pp is a heterozygous purple plant.

Incomplete Dominance

In genetics, a relationship in which neither trait is dominant, and the offspring is a blend of both traits.

Example:
A red flower (AA) is crossed with a white flower (aa). A pink flower (Aa) is created (a mix of red and white).

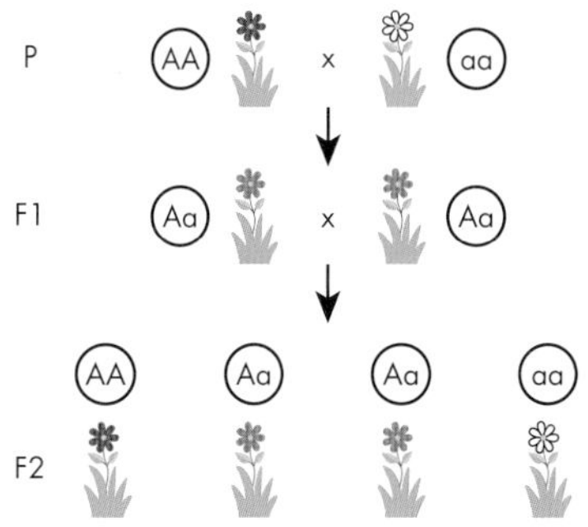

Inherited Trait

Traits that come from a parent or other ancestor.

Examples:
Eye or hair color

Insect

An arthropod that has six legs, compound eyes, a pair of antennae, and a three-part body made up of a head, thorax, and abdomen.

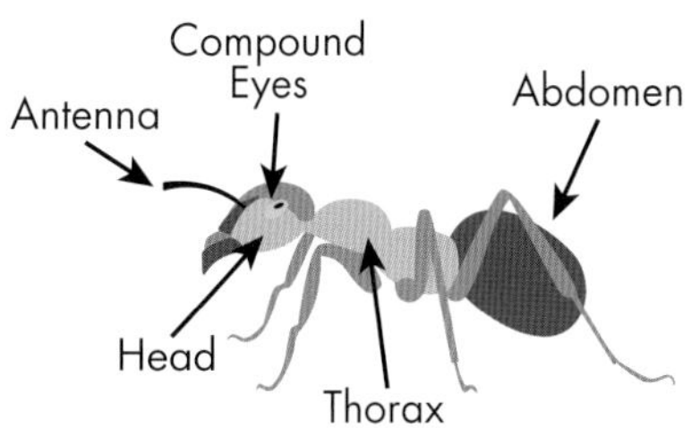

Instinct

A behavior that an organism is born with and does without thinking or training.

Example:
Birds migrating south for the winter

Interphase

The phase of mitosis where the cell is resting. Growth and maturing are taking place during this phase.

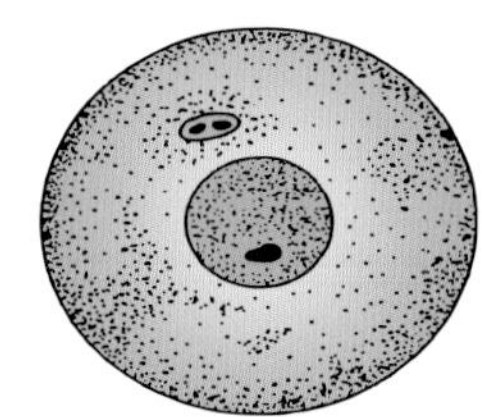

Invertebrates

Animals that do not have a backbone.

Examples:
Jellyfish, insects, spiders, clams, starfish, ants

Kingdom

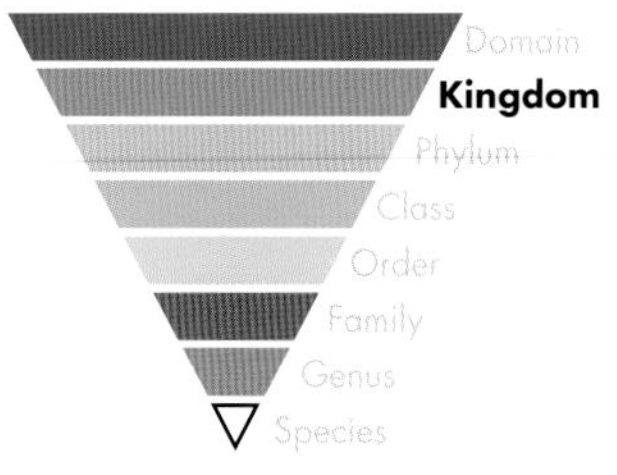

A top layer of classification between domain and phylum.

Learned Behavior

An action or set of actions that an organism learns and changes based on its experiences.

Examples:
Tying your shoes, or when a cat comes to the sound of the can opener as a can of food is opened

Levels of Ecological Organization

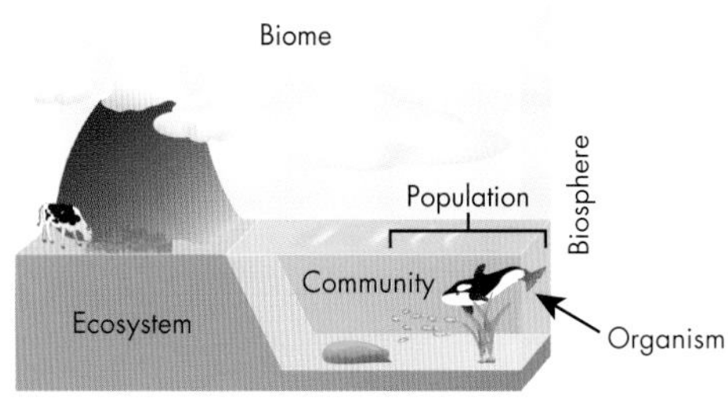

Organization of groupings of living things from simplest to most complex. The levels progress from organism to population, community, ecosystem, biome, and biosphere.

Levels of Organization (Living Things)

Organization of living things from simplest to most complex.

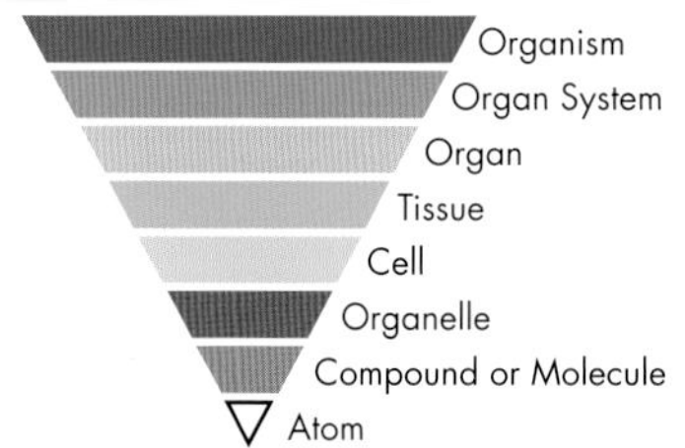

Life Cycle

The life sequence of any organism as it passes from egg to adult.

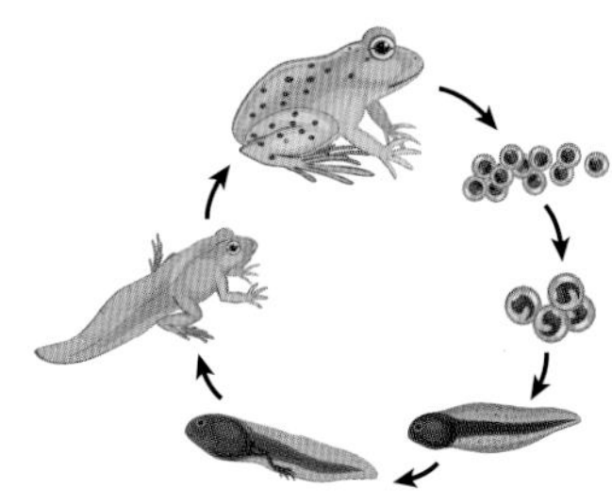

Limiting Factor

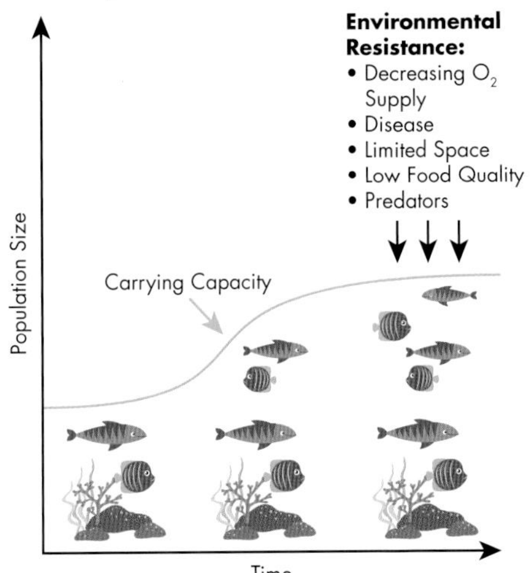

A biotic or abiotic environmental factor that limits the number of individuals in a population. Limiting may be based on food, water, space, and shelter.

Example:
If a desert gets too much rain, the roots of the cacti will rot and the number of cacti will go down.

Living Thing

All living things have seven characteristics:

1. They move.
2. They respond to their environment.
3. They grow and change.
4. They reproduce.
5. They are made of cells.
6. They obtain energy from food.
7. They get rid of waste.

Lysosome

An organelle in a cell that digests food particles, old organelles, and other cellular waste.

Mammals

Animals that are warm-blooded, have body hair, and provide milk for their young. There are three groups: marsupials, monotremes, and placentals.

Examples:
Kangaroos, elephants, anteaters, bats

Marsupials

Mammals whose young stay in pouches for the first part of their life.

Examples:
Koalas, kangaroos

Meiosis

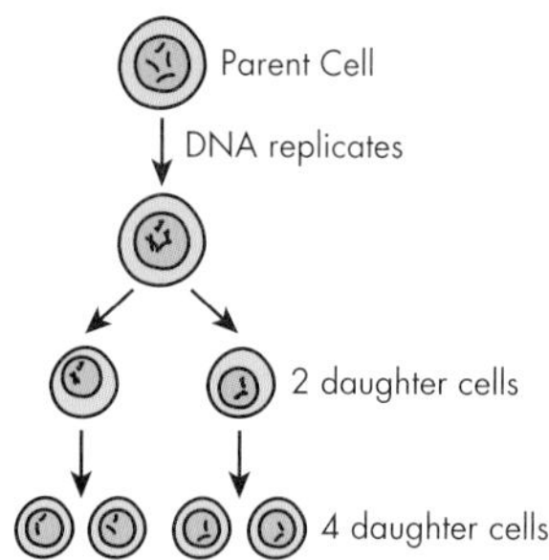

The process of cell division in which a parent cell divides and produces four daughter cells (sex cells) that have half of the chromosomes of the parent.

Metamorphosis

When an organism transforms from egg to adult through distinctly different body structures. Butterflies and moths go through four phases: egg, larva, pupa, and adult.

Metaphase

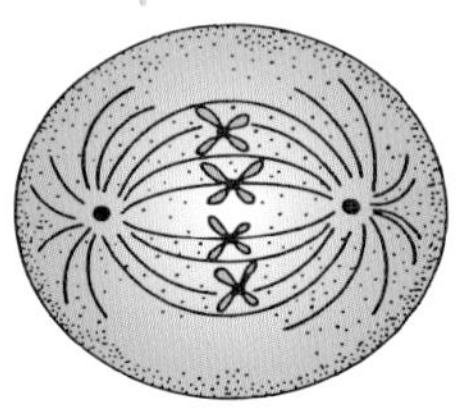

The phase of mitosis where the chromosomes line up in the middle of the cell.

Migration

A large-scale movement of a population.

Examples:
Wildebeests, geese, and monarch butterflies migrate.

Mimicry

When one organism looks like another organism, helping it survive in its environment.

Coral Snake

Scarlet King Snake

Example:
The harmless scarlet king snake (red with yellow and black stripes, in which the red color is next to the black stripes) resembles the poisonous coral snake (red, black, and yellow stripes, but the red is next to the yellow stripes). Predators leave the scarlet king snake alone because it resembles the poisonous coral snake.

Mitochondria

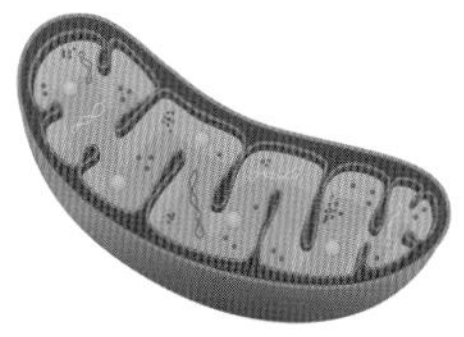

An organelle found in the cytoplasm of cell that helps the cell convert food into usable energy.

Mitosis

The process of cell division in which a parent cell divides and produces two identical daughter cells, each with the same number of chromosomes as the parent cell.

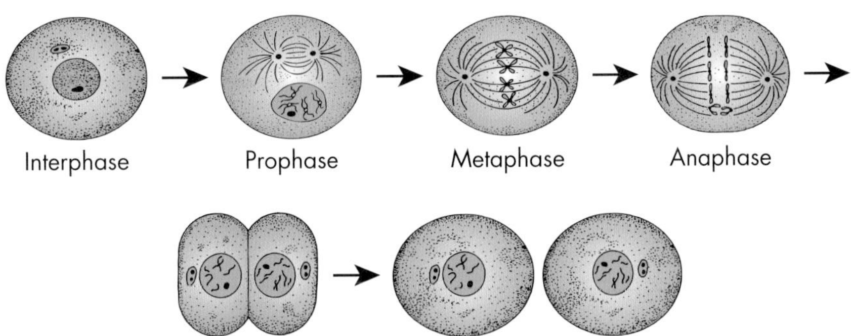

Monotremes

Mammals that lay eggs.

Examples:
Anteaters, duck-billed platypus

Mutation

A permanent change in an organism's DNA.

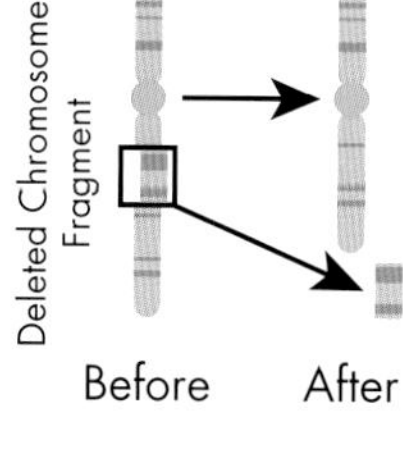

Mutualism

A symbiotic relationship in which both organisms benefit from the relationship.

Example:
Clownfish benefit from the protection of sea anemones, while the sea anemones benefit by eating the larger fish the clownfish attract as well as the clownfish's scraps.

Natural Selection

The idea that if an organism has characteristics or traits that help it survive better in its environment, it will survive to produce more offspring than other organisms that do not have the helpful trait. This will lead to the helpful trait becoming more and more evident in future generations.

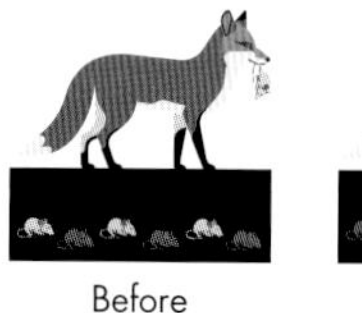

Before

After

Niche

The special area or function an organism has in its habitat.

Nitrogen Cycle

The steps by which nitrogen is taken out of soil and water by living things and ultimately returned to the soil.

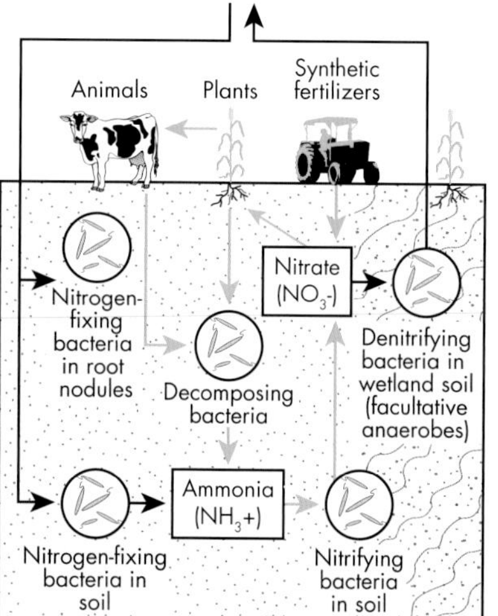

Nucleus

The control center for the cell that contains the genetic material, DNA.

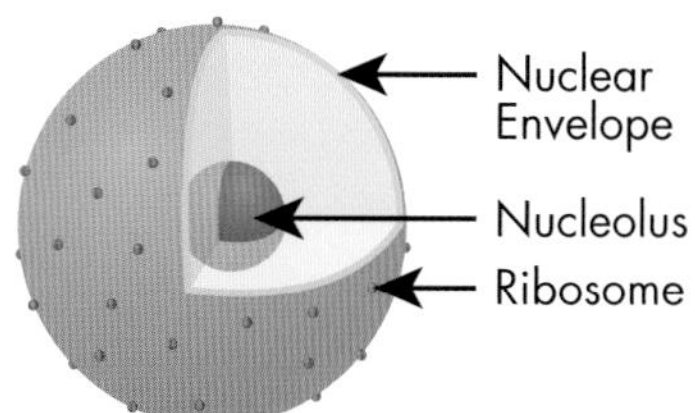

Omnivore

An organism that eats both plants and animals as its food source.

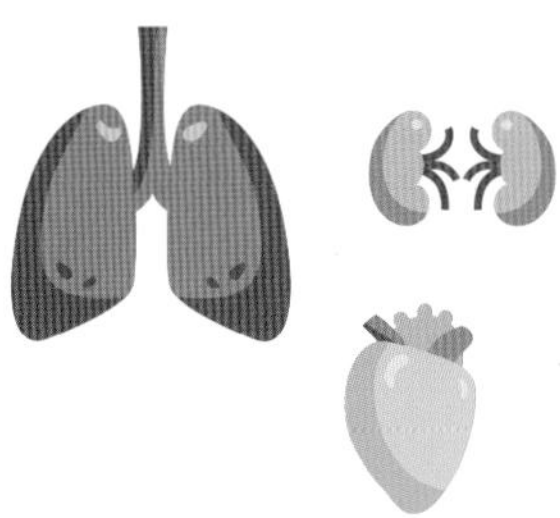

Organ

A part of an organism that performs a specific function.

Organelle

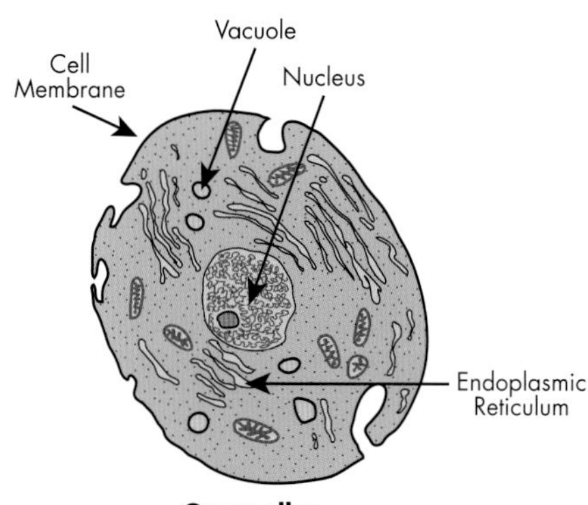

Organelles

A structure in the cell that has a specific function.

Examples:
Cell wall, cell membrane, nucleus, cytoplasm, nuclear membrane, endoplasmic reticulum, ribosome, mitochondrion, vacuole, lysosome, chloroplast

Organism

A living thing.

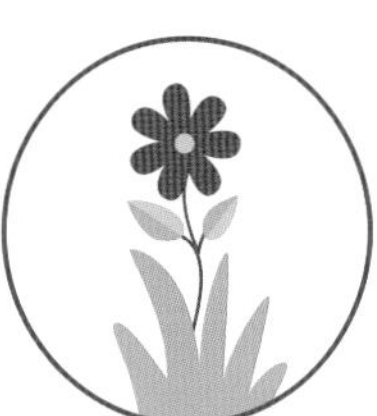

Organ System

A group of organs in the human body that work together to carry out a vital function.

System	Organs	Main Function(s)
Circulatory	Heart, blood vessel, blood	Moving of materials through the body
Digestive	Mouth, pharynx, esophagus, stomach, intestine, liver, pancreas, anus	Processing of food, chewing, digesting, nutrient absorbing, and waste eliminating
Endocrine	Pituitary, thyroid, pancreas, adrenal	Coordinating different body functions (such as digestion)
Excretory	Ureters, kidneys, urinary bladder, urethra	Removing wastes from blood and ultimately the body
Integumentary	Skin	Protecting from injury and infection
Lymphatic	Bone marrow, lymph nodes, thymus, spleen, lymph vessels, white blood cells	Defending from infections within the body
Muscular	Skeletal muscles	Allowing different part of the body to move
Nervous	Brain, spinal cord, nerves, sense organs	Coordinating all of the body's activities
Respiratory	Lungs, trachea	Facilitating the gas exchange between the body and its environment
Skeletal	Skeleton, ligaments, tendons, cartilage	Supporting the body, protecting the internal organs, and allowing for movement

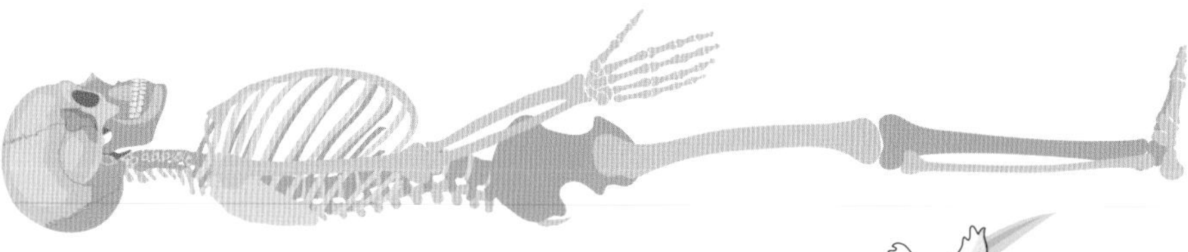

Ovary

The part of a flowering plant that contains the seeds. It will mature into a fruit.

Parasitism

A symbiotic relationship in which one organism benefits from the relationship and the other organism is harmed.

Example:
A dog and its fleas

Petals

The brightly colored parts of the flower that surround and help protect the reproductive parts of the flower.

Phenotype

The way an organism looks based on its genetic makeup or alleles.

Example:
The phenotype for a plant with a genotype of Pp would be purple.

Phenotypic Ratio

The ratio of the phenotypes of predicted offspring using a Punnett square.

	Phenotype		Genotype	
3	Purple		*PP* (homozygous)	1
	Purple		*Pp* (heterozygous)	2
	Purple		*Pp* (heterozygous)	
1	White		*pp* (homozygous)	1
	Ratio 3:1		Ratio 1:2:1	

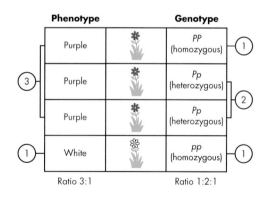

Example:
By using a Punnett square, you can calculate that the four possible offspring would be: PP (purple), Pp (purple), Pp (purple), and pp (white). The phenotypic ratio for this would be 3:1, or 3 purple plants for every 1 white plant.

Phloem

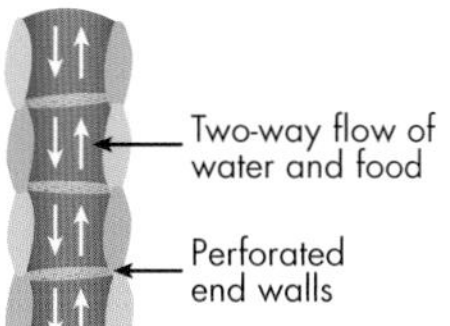

The tissue in the stem of the plant that transports the food and nutrients throughout the plant.

LIFE SCIENCES

Photosynthesis

The process in which plants use sunlight to combine carbon dioxide and water to create food. Its chemical formula is:

$6\ CO_2 + 6\ H_2O + \text{energy} \rightarrow 6\ O_2 + C_6H_{12}O_6$

carbon dioxide + water + sunlight → oxygen + carbohydrate (sugar)

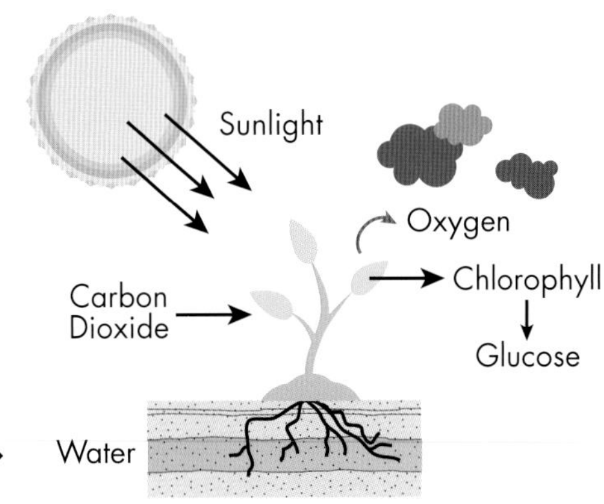

Phylogenetic Tree

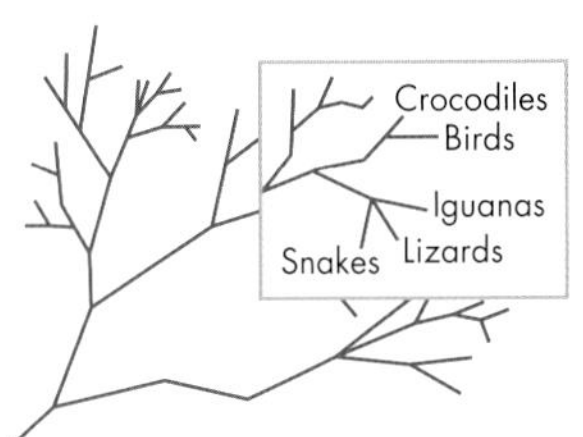

A diagram that represents how scientists believe organisms may be related to other organisms.

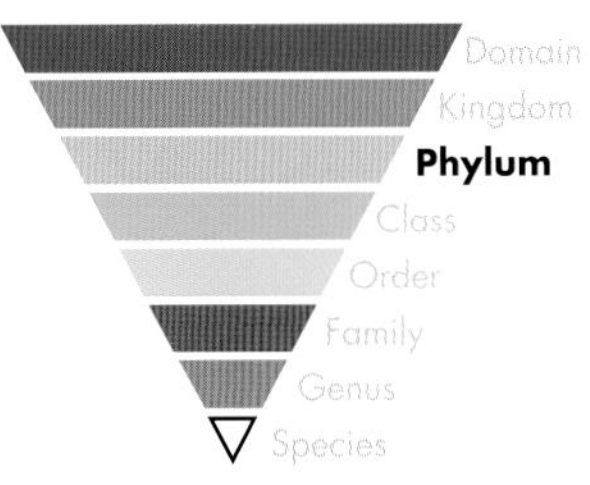

Phylum

A level of classification between Kingdom and Class.

Pistil

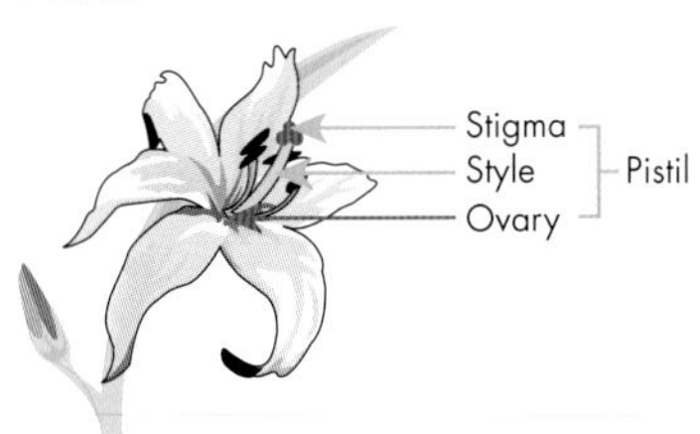

The female reproductive parts of a flowering plant. It includes the stigma, style, and ovary.

Pollen

The main reproductive cells in most plants, produced by the anther.

Prey

An animal that is hunted or caught for food.

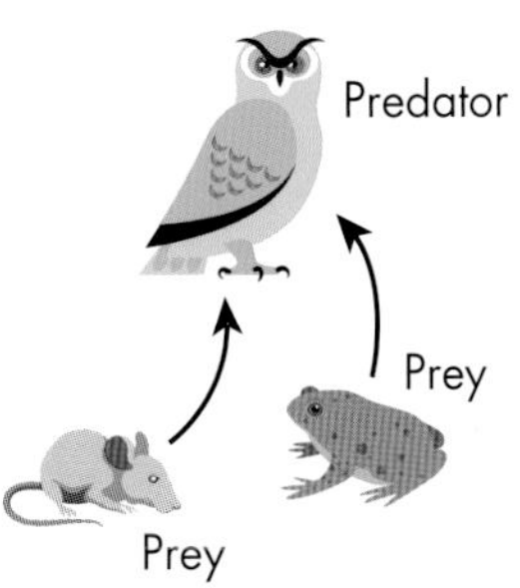

Producer

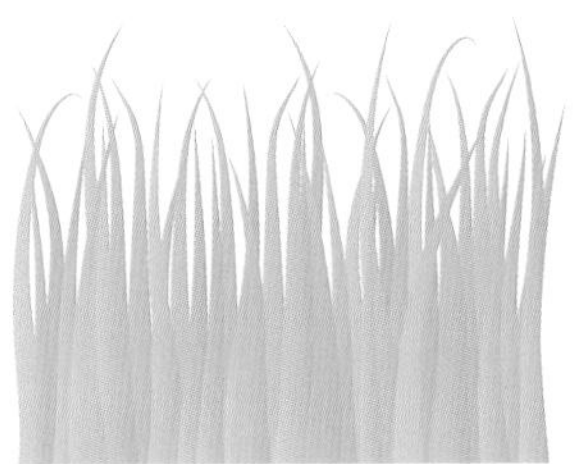

An organism that produces its own food and is a food for other organisms; usually a green plant.

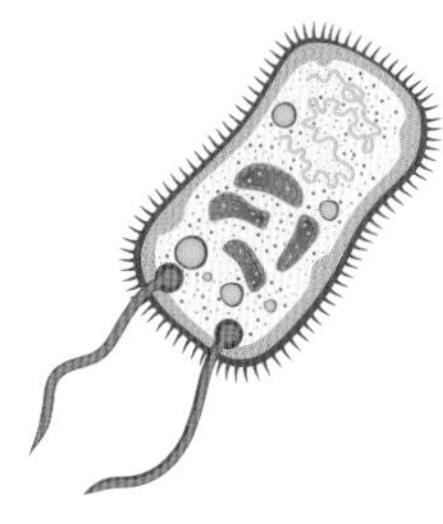

Prokaryote

A single-celled organism that does not have a distinct nucleus or specialized organelles.

Prophase

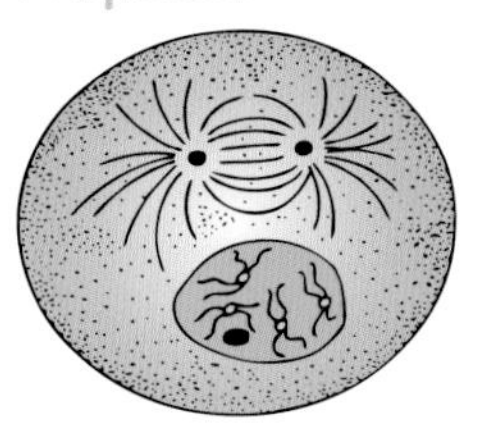

The phase of mitosis where chromosomes copy themselves and the nucleus starts to disappear.

Punnett Square

A method used to predict the outcomes of genetic crosses.

	T	t
T	TT	Tt
t	Tt	tt

Purebred

Another term for having homozygous alleles for a certain trait.

Examples:
PP is a purebred, or homozygous purple flower, or pp would be a purebred white flower.

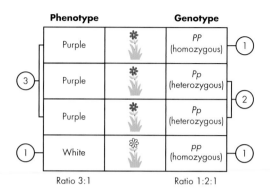

	Phenotype		Genotype	
3	Purple		*PP* (homozygous)	1
	Purple		*Pp* (heterozygous)	2
	Purple		*Pp* (heterozygous)	
1	White		*pp* (homozygous)	1
	Ratio 3:1		Ratio 1:2:1	

Recessive Trait

A trait that must be contributed by both parents in order to appear in the offspring. It will always be overridden by the dominant trait. Its allele is shown by using a lowercase letter.

Example:
A short plant would have the genotype pp because tall is dominant (P).

Reptile

A group of cold-blooded animals that have scales, breathe air, and usually lay eggs.

Examples:
Turtles, lizard, snakes, crocodiles, alligators

Respiration

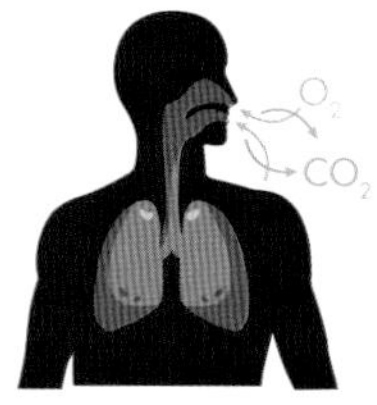

The way that an organism exchanges gasses with its environment.

Ribosome

An organelle where protein synthesis takes place. It is found either in the cytoplasm of a cell or on an endoplasmic reticulum.

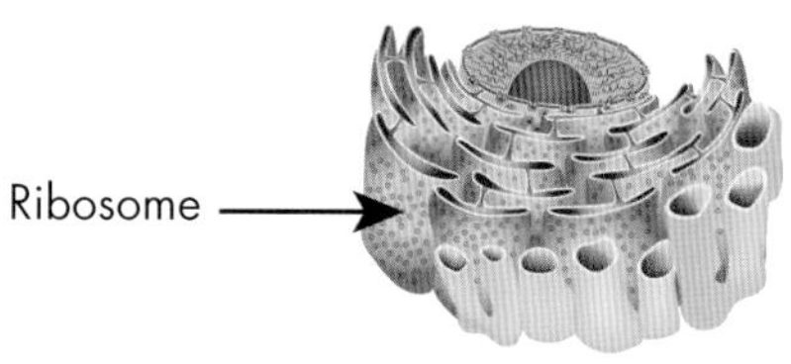

RNA (Ribonucleic Acid)

A long single strand of nucleic acid that assists a cell in making proteins.

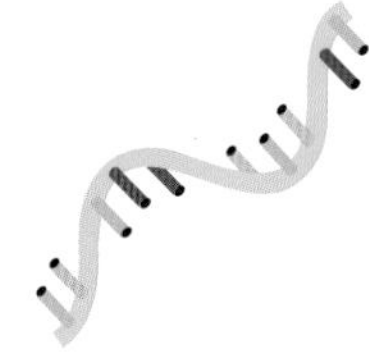

Scavenger

An organism that feeds on dead or decaying animals.

Examples:
Leopards, raccoon, coyotes, vultures

Sepal

A modified leaf, sometimes looking like a petal, that is found at the base of the flower blossom.

Species

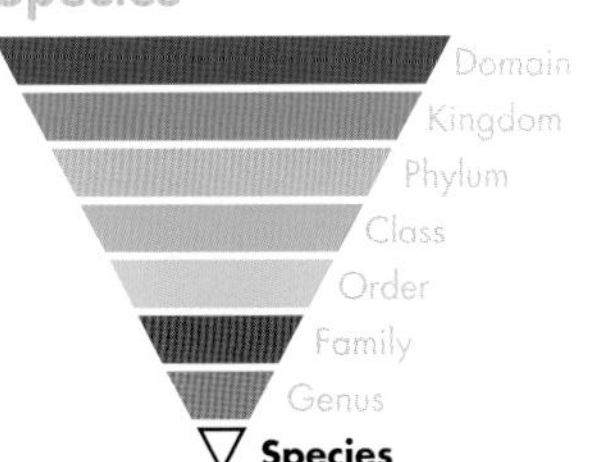

The most specialized level of classification.

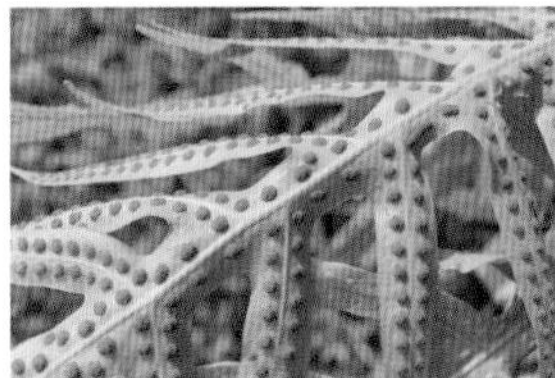

Spore

A reproductive cell made by plants and fungi.

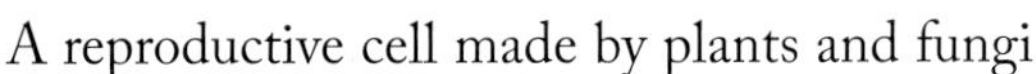

Stamen

The male reproductive parts of a flowering plant. It includes the anther and the filament.

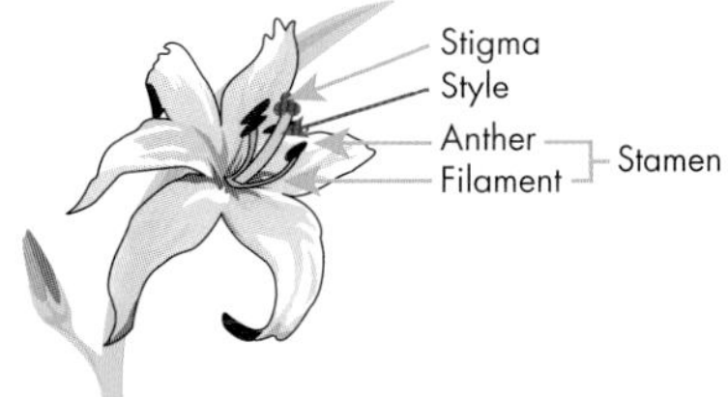

Stigma

The part of the female reproductive system in flowering plants that receives the pollen from the anthers. It is located at the top or end of the style.

Style

This female reproductive organ in flowering plants connects the stigma with the ovary.

Succession

The processes a community goes through as it changes over time. There two different types: primary (the development of a new ecosystem starting with soil development) and secondary (started by an event that impacts an established ecosystem).

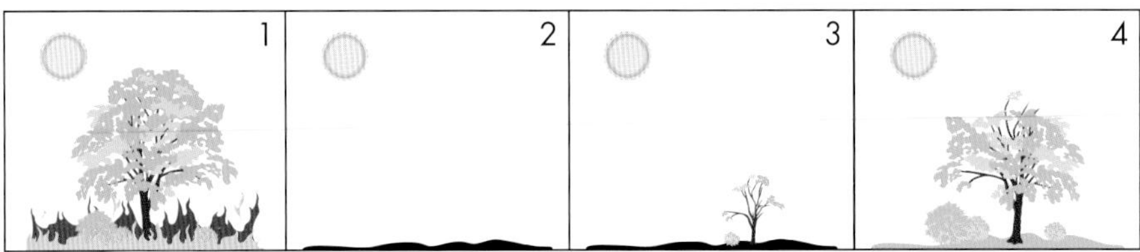

Symbiosis

Relationship between two living things. These relationships could be beneficial to one (commensalism), beneficial to both (mutualism), or harmful to one (parasitism).

Commensalism

Mutualism

Parasitism

Taiga

A biome where it snows and has cone-producing trees, like pines and spruces.

Telephase

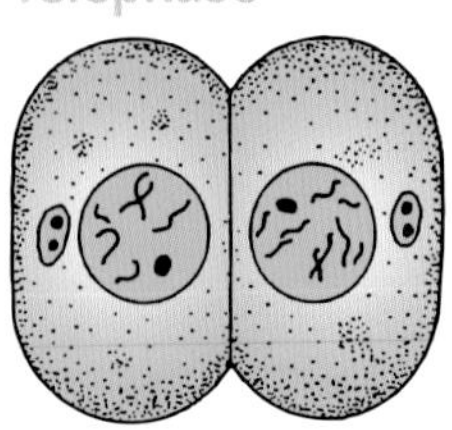

The phase of mitosis where the division between the two new cells forms.

Temperate Rain Forest

A biome in a moderate temperature zone with heavy rainfall and cone-bearing or large-leafed trees.

Tissue

A group of similar cells that work together to perform a specific function for an organism.

Examples:
Muscle, nerve, connective, epidermal

Muscle Tissue

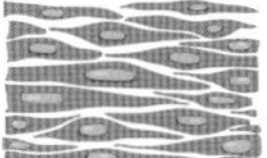

Smooth

Skeletal

Cardiac

Trait

A feature or characteristic of an organism.

Transpiration

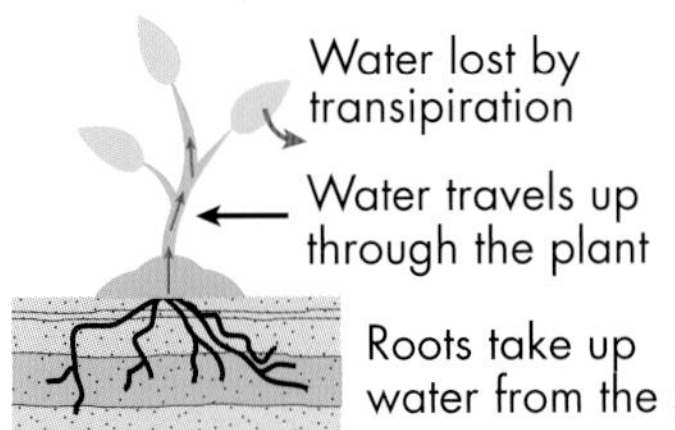
Water lost by transipiration
Water travels up through the plant
Roots take up water from the soil

A process in plants in which they lose water through the undersides of their leaves.

Tropical Rain Forest

A biome located within 10 degrees north or south of the equator. The area receives at least 100 inches of rain each year.

Tropism

When an organism (usually a plant) moves toward or away from something.

Example:
Plants grow toward sunlight or heat; hang a plant upside down and it will grow upright.

Tundra

A biome without trees that remains permanently frozen throughout the year.

Vacuole

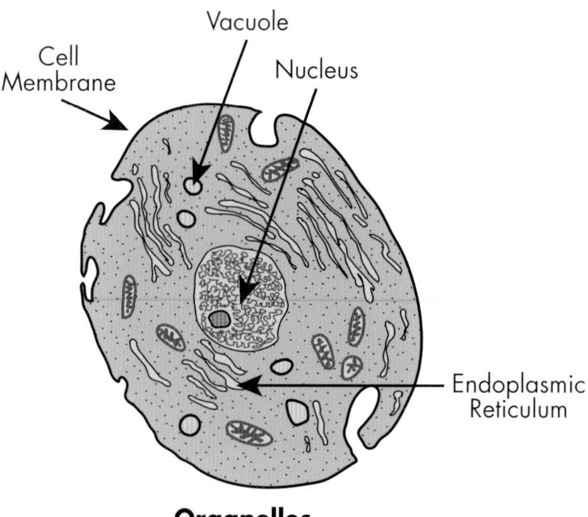

Organelles

An organelle found in the cytoplasm of cells that is used to store water or nutrients. It usually is quite large in plant cells and smaller in animal cells.

Vertebrates

Animals that have a backbone.

Examples:
Humans, dogs, horses, fish, reptiles, birds, amphibians, frogs

Vestigial Structures

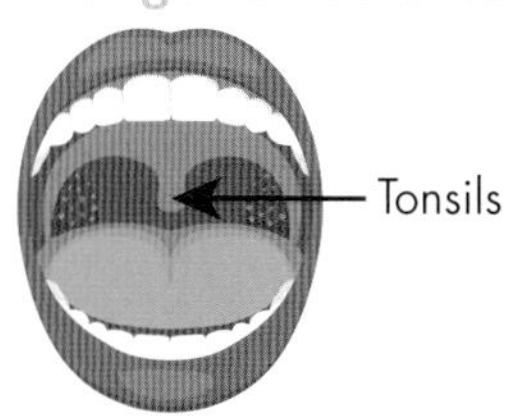

Structures or organs that no longer have an important function for an organism.

Examples:
Appendix, tonsils

Virus

A microscopic nonliving structure that can infect living things. Their basic structure includes nucleic acid (DNA/RNA) and a protein coat. There are two different life cycles: the lytic and the lysogenic.

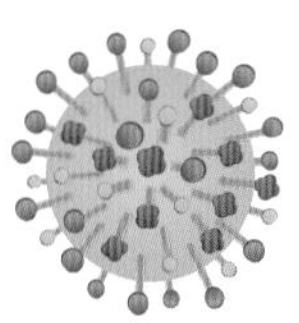

Influenza

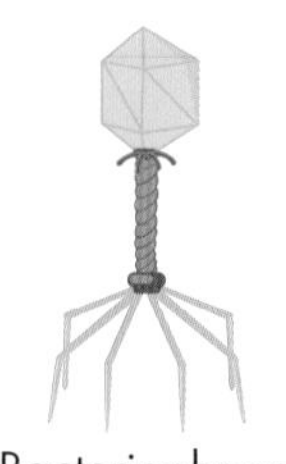

Bacteriophage

Warm-Blooded

An organism that can maintain a relatively constant body temperature no matter its environment.

Xylem

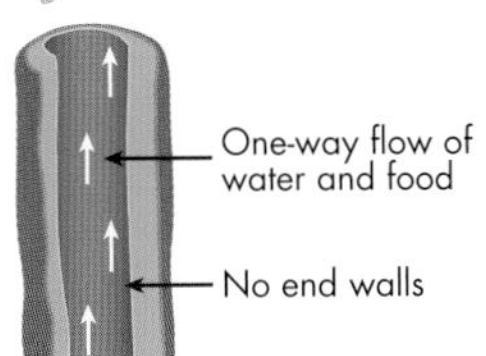

The tissue in the stem of the plant that transports water throughout the plant and helps support it.

Zygote

A cell formed from two cells—one from the mother and one from the father; the first cell of an offspring.

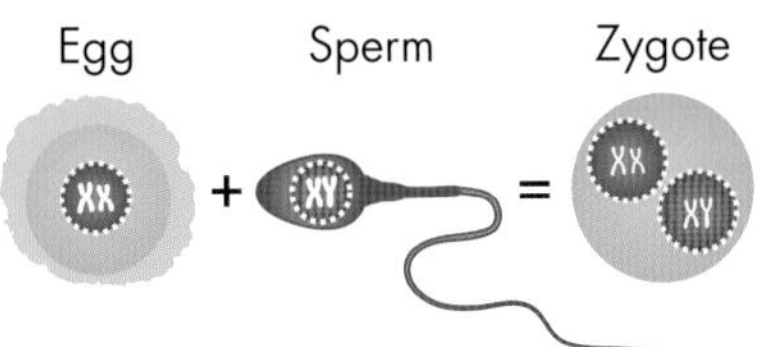

PHYSICAL SCIENCES

Absorption

When a substance absorbs waves that hit it.

Examples:
Soundproof material absorbing sound, or black surfaces absorbing light.

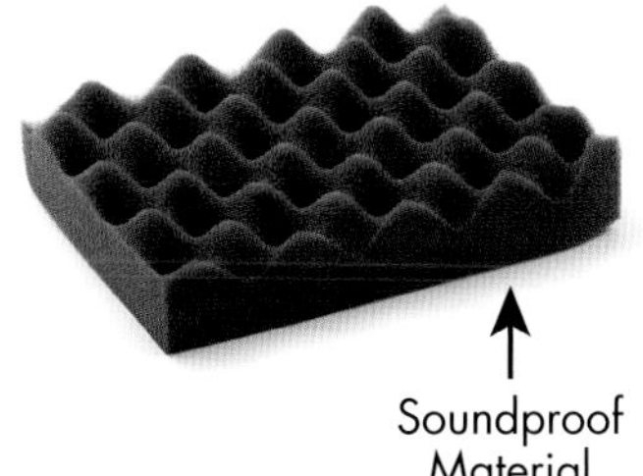

Acceleration

The amount velocity changes in a certain amount of time. Usually expressed in m/sec^2. A negative acceleration means the object is slowing down.

Calculating Acceleration:

★ Use the formula: $A = \frac{V_f - V_i}{t}$

- A = acceleration
- V_f = the final velocity
- V_i = the initial or starting velocity
- t = the time for the acceleration to take place

Acid

A material that has a pH less than 7. It turns blue litmus paper red.

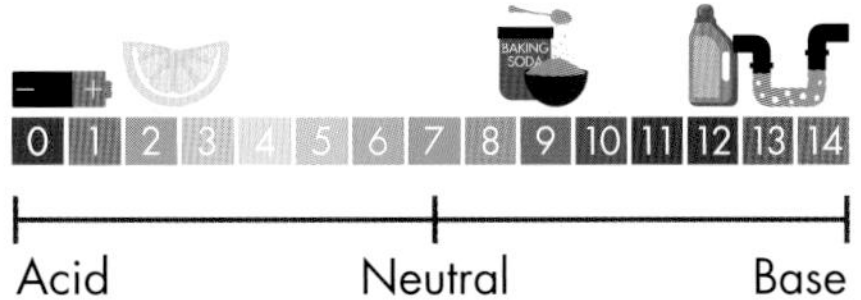

Examples:
Citric acid (found in sodas and lemon juice), battery acid

Action-Reaction Pair

The basis for Newton's third law of motion. A pair of motions in which one is the initial action and the other is the reaction to the initial action.

Amplitude

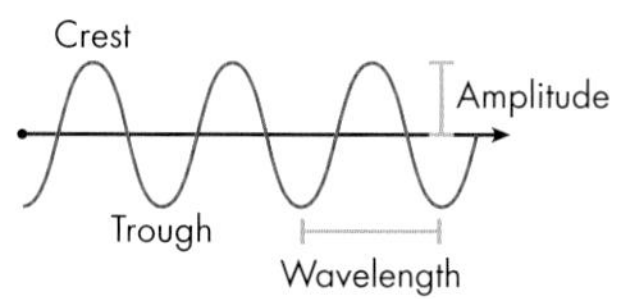

In a transverse wave, the distance from the rest position of wave to the crest (top) or trough (bottom). In a compressional wave, it is the distance from the rest position to a compression (area of compacted medium) or rarefaction (area of spread-out medium).

Atom

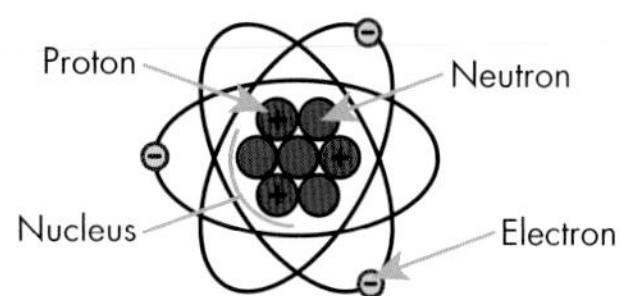

The smallest piece of an element. Made up of a nucleus and a cloud of electrons.

Atomic Mass

The total mass of an atom; the number of protons and neutrons in an atom. Shown by the unit u, or the unified atomic mass unit.

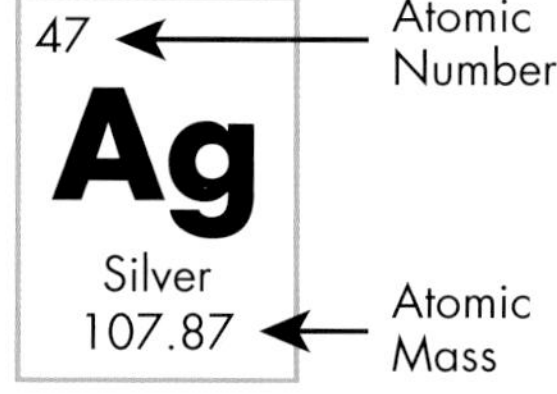

Example:
Silver's atomic mass is 107.87 u.

Atomic Number

The number of protons in an atomic nucleus.

Average Speed

An average of the speed traveled throughout the entire trip. It is calculated by dividing the total distance by the total amount of time the trip took to complete.

Calculating Average Speed: $S_{average} = \frac{\text{total distance}}{\text{total time}}$

Base

A material that has a pH greater than 7. It turns red litmus paper blue.

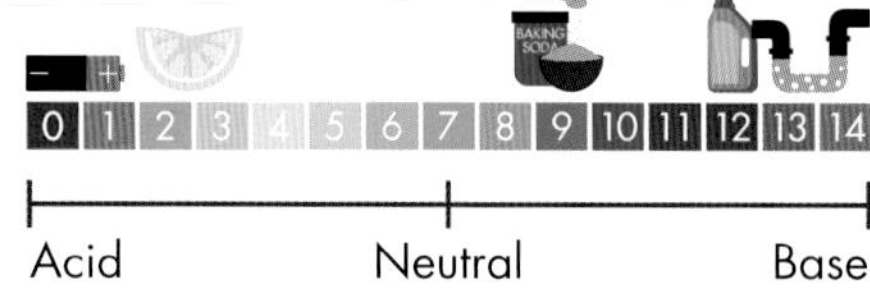

Examples:
Baking soda, drain cleaner

Bohr Model

A model that shows the approximate location of the protons, neutrons, and electrons in an atom, with the electrons traveling in orbits around the nucleus.

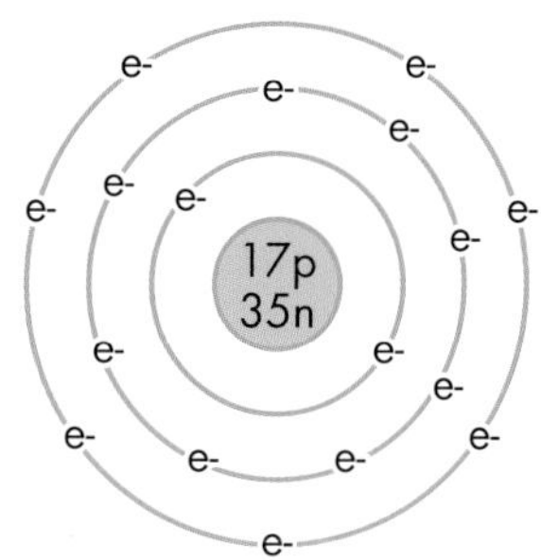

Boiling Point

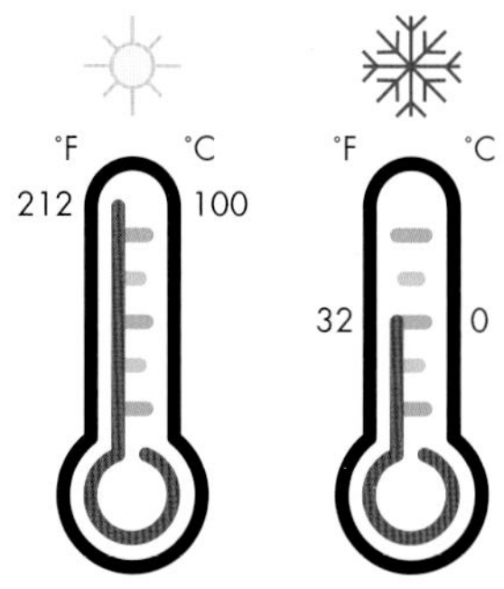

The temperature at which a liquid boils. Water boils at 100°C or 212°F.

Buoyancy

The capacity to float in either air or liquid. The principal of buoyancy, which states that for an object to float it must displace enough of the fluid around it, is attributed to Archimedes.

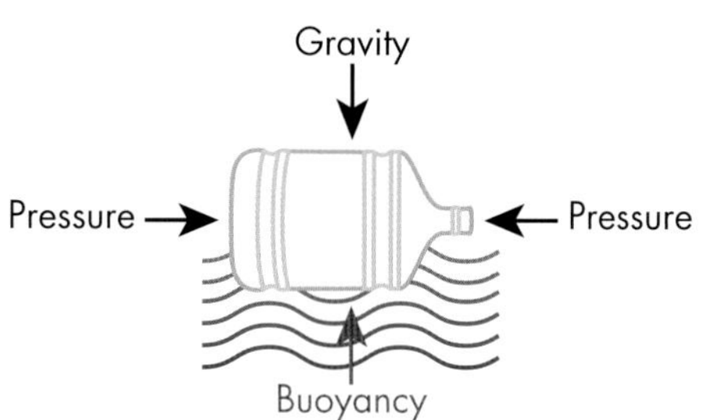

Chemical Change (Chemical Reaction)

Any change that creates a new substance by altering the chemical makeup of a compound. Evidence of a chemical change could be change in temperature, light, heat, or sound given off, or the formation of gasses.

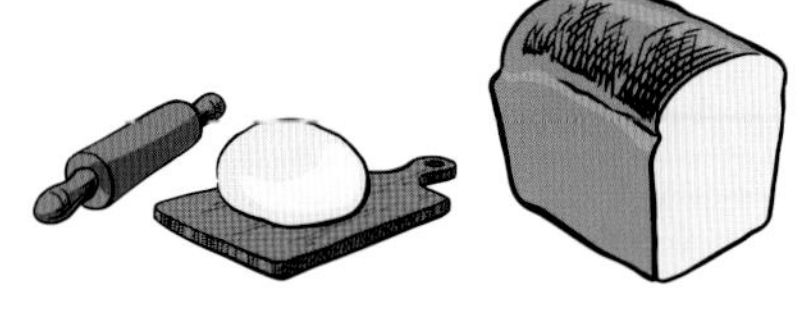

Examples:
Combustion (wood burning), oxidation (iron rusting), cooking (or baking)

Chemical Formula

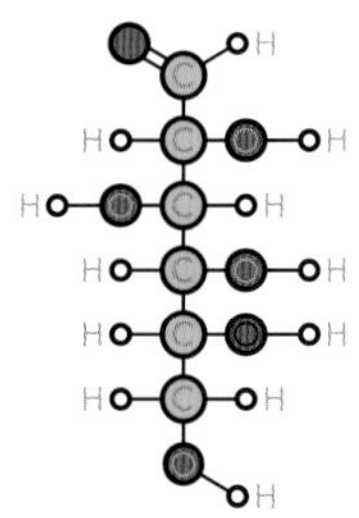

A written representation of a chemical substance containing letters that represent elements from the periodic table and subscripts (numbers written lower than the letters) that show the number of each element.

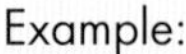

Example:
Glucose has a chemical formula of $C_6H_{12}O_6$ which means it is made up of six carbon atoms, 12 hydrogen atoms, and six oxygen atoms.

Chemical Property

A property of a substance that can be observed during a chemical change.

Example:
Combustibility (ability to burn), reactivity (with other elements)

Chemical Symbol

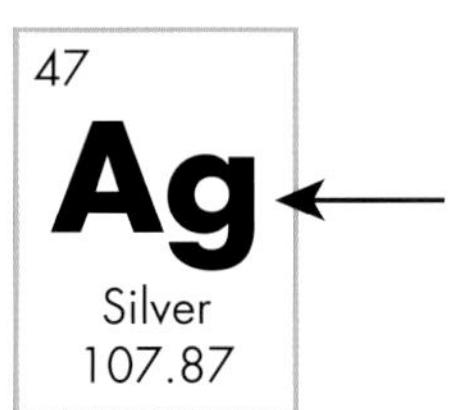

A one- or two-letter symbol that represents an element. Sometimes the symbols are logical, such as O for Oxygen or C for Carbon. The symbols may not always be as obvious, such as Pb for Lead (which in Latin is **p**lum**b**um) or Sn for Tin (which in Latin is **s**ta**n**num).

Circuit

A closed path that electricity follows. There are two basic types: series and parallel.

Combustibility

How easily a material will ignite or burn. It also is a chemical property.

Compound

A substance made up of two or more elements that cannot be separated by a physical change.

Examples:
Salt (NaCl), water (H_2O), sugar ($C_{12}H_{22}O_{11}$)

Concentration

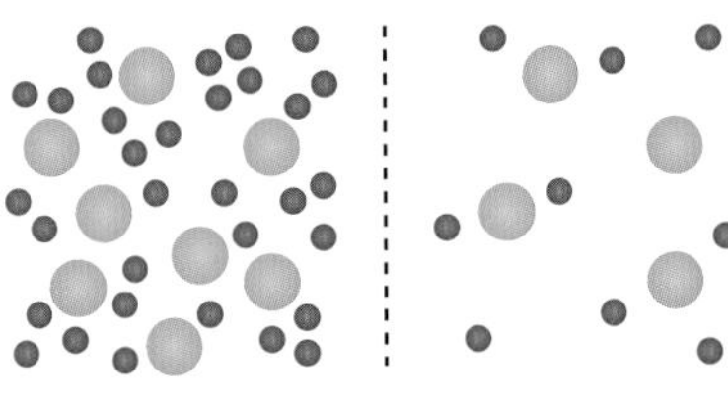

The amount of a substance (solute) compared to what is it is dissolved in (solvent).

Conductivity

The ability of an object to conduct or transmit heat, electricity, or sound.

Conductor

A material that can allow heat, light, sound, or electricity to pass through it easily.

Example:
Metal is a good conductor of heat and electricity because it transmits them so easily.

Crest

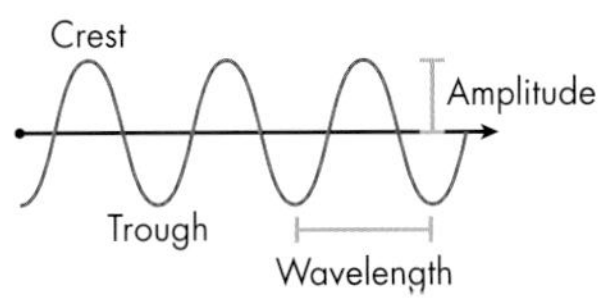

The top of a transverse wave.

Current

The rate of flow of electrons (electric charges) or water. Electric current is measured in Amperes (A).

Calculating Current Given the Resistance:

- ★ Use Ohm's Law formula: $I = \frac{V}{R}$
  - I = current (amps)
  - V = voltage (volts)
  - R = resistance (ohms Ω)

Current, continued

Calculating Current Given the Power:

★ Use Ohm's Law formula: $I = \frac{P}{V}$
- I = current (amps)
- P = power (watts)
- V = voltage (volts)

Density

A measure of the compactness of the molecules of a material. The closer the particles are to one another, the higher the density of the material. The mass per unit of volume of a material.

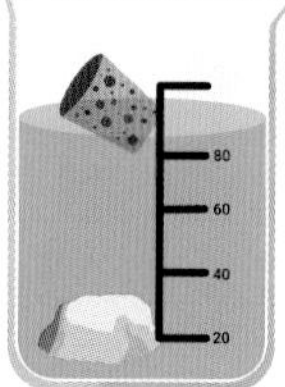

Calculating Density:

★ Use the formula: $D = \frac{m}{v}$
- D = density
- m = mass
- v = volume

Deposition

When a gas changes to a solid.

Example:
When frost forms on the ground or windows, it is water vapor changing to ice.

Diatomic Molecule

A molecule that is made up of two atoms. It always will be bonded with another atom, even it is more of the same kind of atom.

Examples:
Hydrogen (H_2), Oxygen (O_2), Fluorine (F_2), Iodine (I_2), Bromine (Br_2), Chlorine (Cl_2), Nitrogen (N_2)

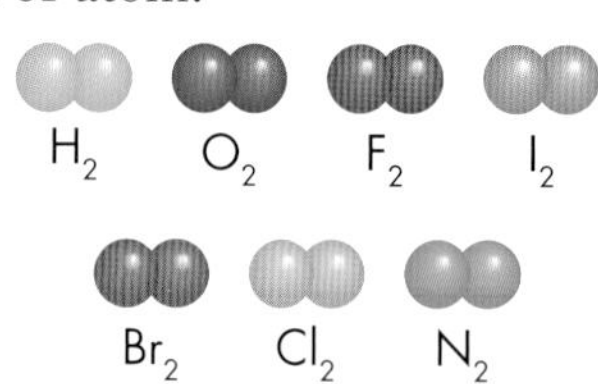

Diffract/Diffraction

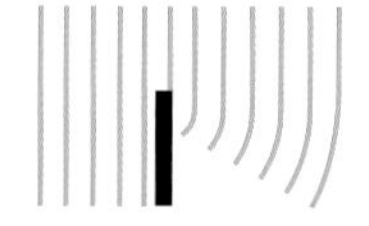

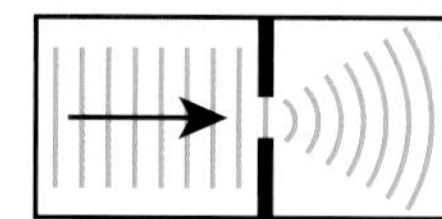

The bending of waves around an obstacle or the spreading of waves as they go through an opening.

Doppler Effect/Doppler Shift

When the frequency of a light or sound wave is changed because the object producing the wave is in motion. In sound, the higher the frequency, the higher the pitch; in light, the higher frequency light is blue while the lower frequency light is red.

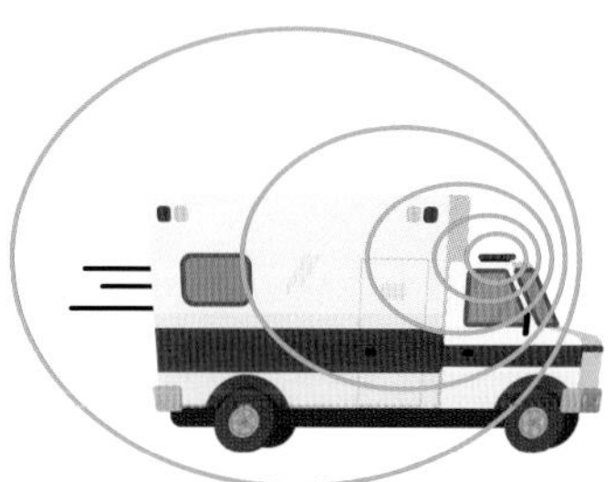

Example:
As an ambulance with its sirens blaring approaches you, the sound waves in front of it are compressed, giving it a higher frequency and therefore a higher pitch. As it passes you, the waves spread out so the frequency is lower and the pitch is lower as well.

Ductile

Can be made into thin wires. This is a property of metals.

Efficiency

A measure of how well a machine converts the energy put in (input) into the work it does (output). It is usually expressed as a percentage, calculated by dividing the output by input.

$$\text{Efficiency} = [\text{Work}_{output} / \text{Work}_{input}] \bullet 100$$

Effort

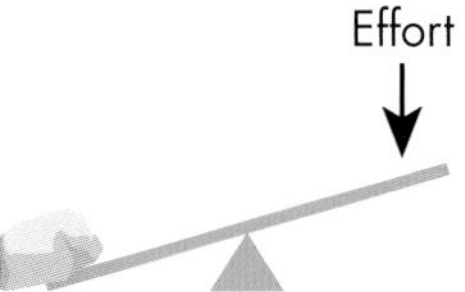

A measure of the amount of work or energy exerted on a machine.

Electromagnet

Wrapped wire around an iron core that acts like a magnet when electric current flows through the wire.

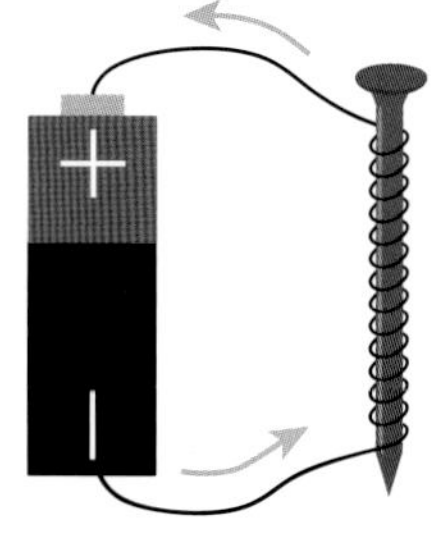

PHYSICAL SCIENCES

Electromagnetic Spectrum

A distribution of electromagnetic radiations that range from longest wavelengths and slowest speeds to shortest wavelengths and fastest speeds.

Examples:
Radio waves, microwaves, infrared waves, visible spectrum, ultraviolet waves, x-rays, and gamma rays

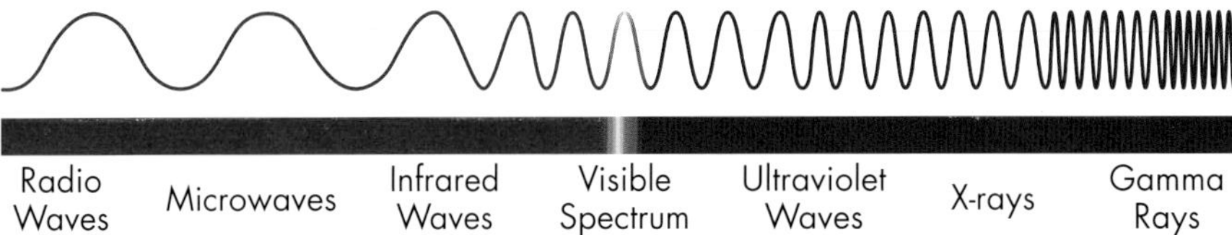

Electrons

Tiny negatively charged participles that move around the nucleus of the atom. Their mass is about 1/1836 of a proton or neutron so they do not calculate into the atomic mass.

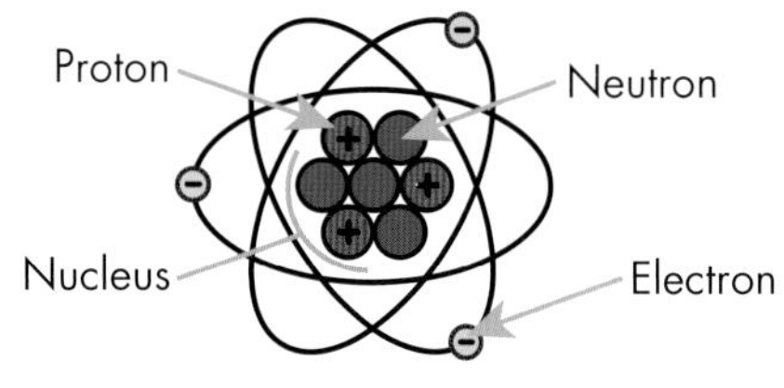

Calculating the Number of Electrons in an Atom:

- In an electrically stable atom, the number of electrons equals the number of protons (atomic number).
- Hydrogen has an atomic number of 1, which means it has one proton and one electron.

Element

A substance made up of all of the same atoms. Found on the periodic table.

Energy

The ability to do work. Measured in joules.

Families

The vertical columns of the periodic table; also called groups. Families have certain common characteristics or traits. There are 18 families in the standard periodic table.

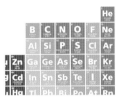

- Noble Gasses
- Halogens
- Nonmetals
- Metalloids
- Other Metals
- Transition Metals

Examples:
Alkali metals, Alkaline Earth metals, halogens, noble gasses

Flammable

A chemical property that means the substance can be burned.

Force

A push or a pull.

Freezing Point

The temperature at which a substance changes from liquid to solid, or freezes.

Frequency

The number of waves that pass a certain point in one second. It is measured in Hertz (Hz).

Calculating Frequency:

★ Use the formula: $F = \frac{v}{\lambda}$

- F = frequency (Hertz)
- v = speed (usually in m/sec)
- λ = wavelength (in meters)

Friction

A force that resists motion when two objects move against each other.

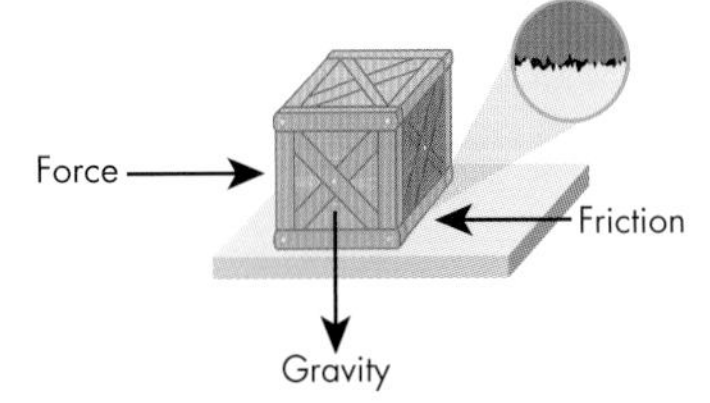

Fulcrum

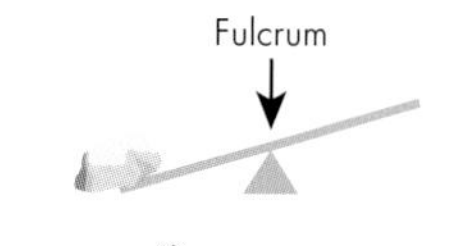

A point that a level or simple machine moves around.

Gamma Rays

The highest energy wave on the electromagnetic spectrum. Only stopped by lead.

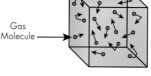

Gas Molecule

Gas

A state of matter that does not have a definite shape or volume. It will fill the container in which it is placed. The particles have high energy and are in motion.

Gravity

A natural force of attraction between bodies in space with great mass and other objects in space as well as the objects on their surfaces. Gravity determines weight. Acceleration due to gravity: 9.8 m/sec^2

Groups

The vertical columns of the periodic table; also called families. Groups have common characteristics or traits. There are 18 groups in the standard periodic table.

Examples:
Alkali metals, Alkaline Earth metals, halogens, noble gasses

Half-Life

The amount of time it takes for half of a radioactive material to decay.

Amount of Time Passed	Percentage of Original Amount That Is Still Present
0 half-lives	100%
1 half-life	50%
2 half-lives	25%
3 half-lives	12.5%

Half-Life, continued

Amount of Time Passed	Percentage of Original Amount That Is Still Present
4 half-lives	6.25%
5 half-lives	3.125%
6 half-lives	1.5625%

Heterogeneous Mixture

A mixture in which the materials are different sizes and often different states of matter. It is easy to tell the difference between the different components in the mixture.

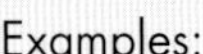

Examples:
Cereal and milk, chicken noodle soup, snack mix, nuts and bolts

Homogeneous Mixture

A mixture in which the different materials appear to be the same state of matter. The particles of the materials in the mixture are similar sizes so the different materials are difficult to tell apart.

Examples:
Powdered drinks in water, saltwater, bronze

Inclined Plane

A simple machine consisting of a sloped surface or ramp used to raise a load.

Calculating the Mechanical Advantage (MA) of an Inclined Plane:

★ Use the formula: $\frac{Distance_{effort}}{Distance_{resistance}}$

- $Distance_{effort}$ = length of the ramp
- $Distance_{resistance}$ = height of the ramp

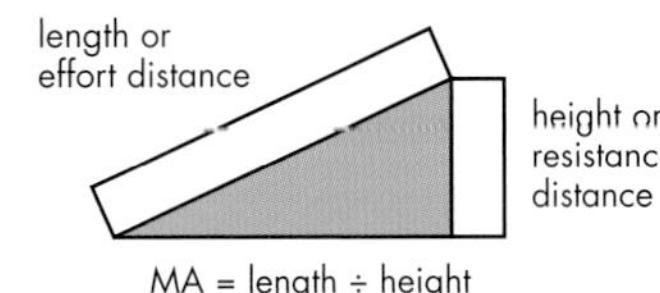

Indicator

Any substance that can show the presence or absence of a chemical or substance.

Examples:
Litmus paper (acids or bases), Hydrion paper (pH)

Inertia (Newton's First Law of Motion)

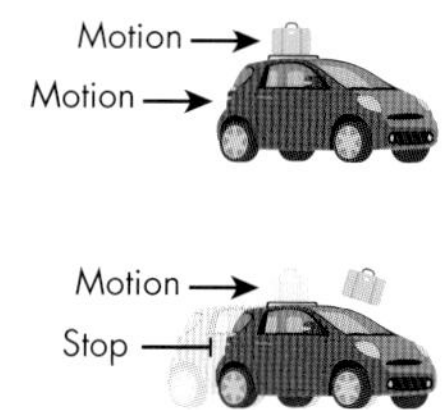

The tendency of a body to resist changing its motion. An object at rest will tend to remain at rest, while an object in motion will tend to remain in motion in a straight line unless acted upon by an outside force.

Examples:
A soccer ball will continue a straight path toward the goal unless blocked. A large rock at the top of a hill will remain where it is unless gravity acts upon it to pull it down.

Infrared Waves

A wave found on the electromagnetic spectrum. Its wavelength is longer than visible light but shorter than microwaves.

Insoluble

A substance that cannot be dissolved in another substance.

Instantaneous Speed

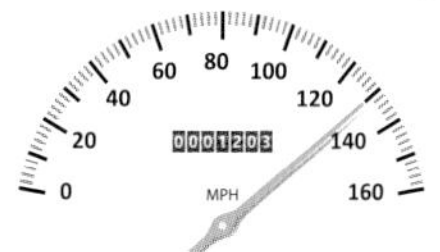

Speed that is measured at an instant in time.

Insulator

Material that slows down or does not allow the passing of heat, light, sound, or electricity.

Example:
Rubber is a good insulator for both electricity and heat.

Interference (Constructive/Destructive)

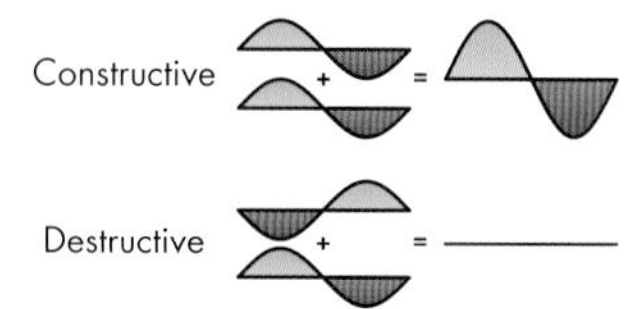

When two waves (light or sound) come together and impact each other. In constructive interference, the troughs and crests meet at the same time, making the wave stronger. In destructive interference, the troughs meet the crests and reduce each other.

Ion

An atom or group of atoms that has acquired a charge because it has gained or lost electrons.

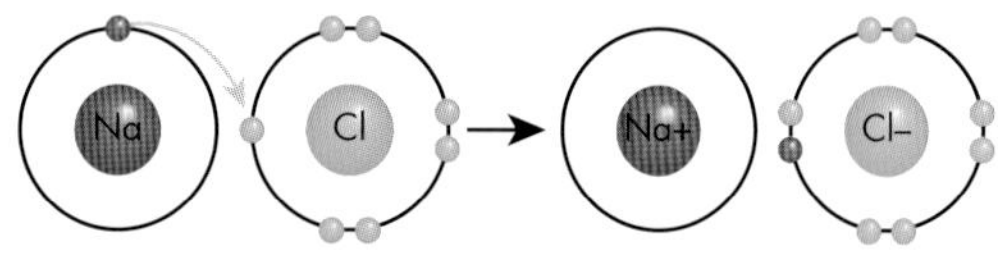

Example:
A hydrogen atom has one proton (one positive charge) and one electron (one negative charge). This makes the atom electrically neutral. When hydrogen loses an electron, it loses one negative so that gives it a total charge of 1 positive. It is a +1 ion.

Isotope

Two atoms that have the same atomic number but different mass numbers, and therefore different numbers of neutrons. It is usually expressed with the element name and its mass (e.g., Carbon–14), and it may be radioactive.

Examples:

- ★ Carbon–12 (its mass matches the periodic table)
  - Atomic Number = 6, so it has 6 protons
  - Atomic Mass = 12, so it has 6 neutrons
- ★ Carbon–14 (it has a mass of 14—does not match the mass written on the periodic table; is an isotope of carbon)
  - Atomic Number = 6, so it has 6 protons
  - Atomic Mass = 14, so it has 8 neutrons

Kinetic Energy

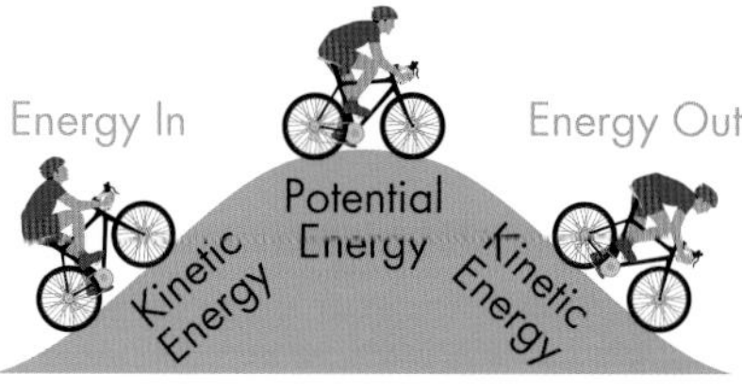

Energy of motion.

Law of Conservation of Energy

A principle that states that energy is neither lost nor gained in any system or energy transfer.

PHYSICAL SCIENCES

Law of Conservation of Mass

A principle that states that mass is neither lost nor gained in any chemical reaction.

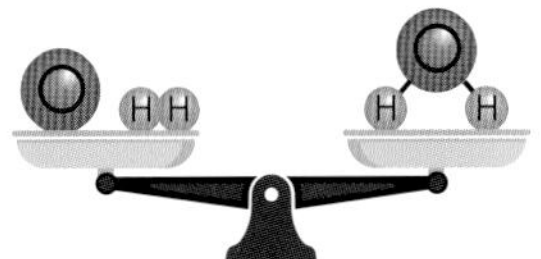

Law of Conservation of Momentum

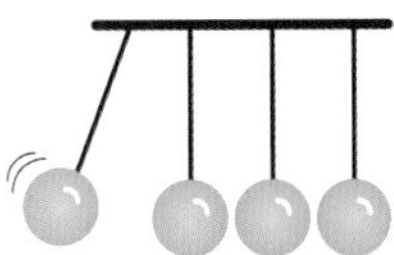

A principle that states that momentum is neither lost nor gained in any system or interaction.

Lever

A simple machine made up of a bar that pivots around a fixed point.

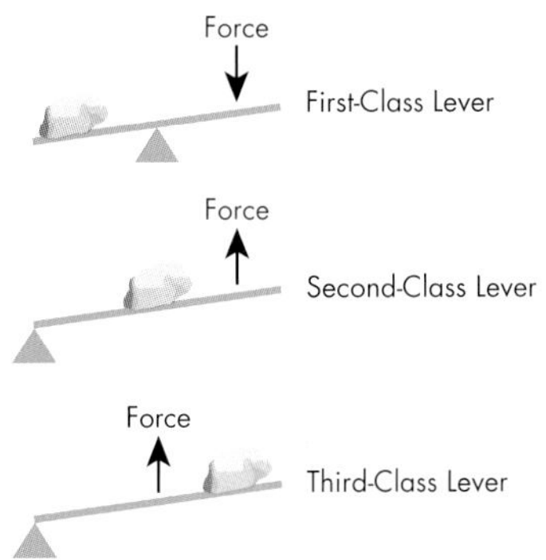

Calculating Mechanical Advantage of a Lever:

★ Use the formula: $\frac{\text{Distance}_{\text{force or effort}}}{\text{Distance}_{\text{load or resistance}}}$

- $\text{Distance}_{\text{force or effort}}$ = measure of the length from the force to the fulcrum
- $\text{Distance}_{\text{load or resistance}}$ = measure of the length from the fulcrum to the load

Liquid

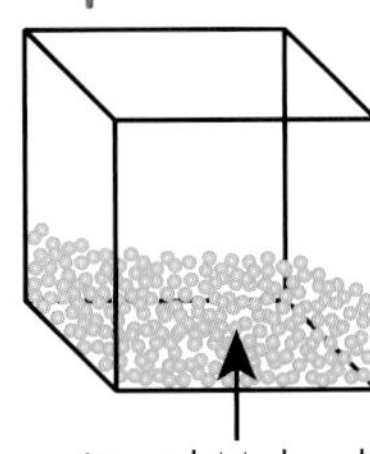

A state of matter with a definite volume but no definite shape. It takes the shape of its container. Its molecules have energy and roll past each other.

Longitudinal (Compressional) Wave

A wave that travels parallel through its medium. The closer the particles of the medium, the faster the longitudinal wave can travel through it.

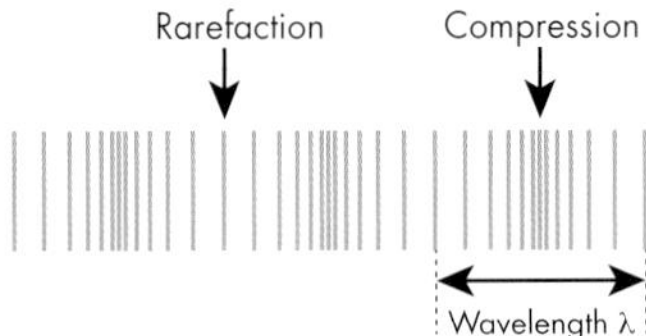

Examples:
Sound waves, earthquake waves

Malleable
Being about to be made into sheets. A property of metals.

Mass
The amount of matter inside an object. It does not change based on gravity. It is usually measured in grams or kilograms.

Matter
Something that has mass and takes up space. It can be solid, liquid, gas, or plasma.

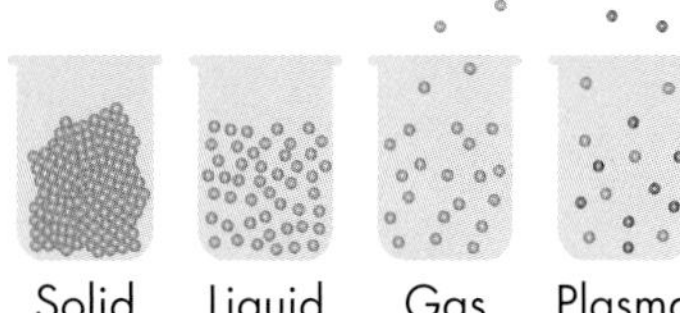

Mechanical Advantage (MA)
The number of times a machine multiplies the force applied to it.

Calculating Mechanical Advantage:

★ Use the formula: $MA = \frac{\text{Resistance Force}}{\text{Effort Force}}$

Melting Point
The temperature at which a solid changes to a liquid. Ice (water) melts at 0°C or 32°F.

Metalloid
An element on the periodic table that has properties of both metals and nonmetals. Located along the stairstep separating the metals from the nonmetals.

Metals
Substances found on the left side of the periodic table. They usually are good conductors of heat and energy.

Microwave
A wave found on the electromagnetic spectrum. It has a shorter wavelength than radio waves, but longer than infrared waves.

Mixture

A combination of one or more substances in which each component retains its own properties and still can be separated. There are two types: heterogeneous mixtures and homogeneous mixtures.

Examples:
Cereal and milk, salad, powdered drinks, snack mix

Molecule

Consisting of two or more atoms joined together, it is the smallest particle of a substance that still has all of the properties of the substance.

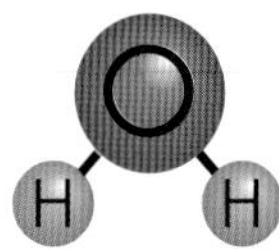

Example:
Water molecule is H_2O, with two atoms of hydrogen and one atom of oxygen.

Momentum

The amount of motion of a moving object.

Calculating Momentum:

★ Use the formula: p = mv
- p = momentum (kg • m/sec)
- m = mass (kg)
- v = velocity (m/sec)

Net Force

A sum of the forces placed on an object. An object has a net force of zero if the object is not moving.

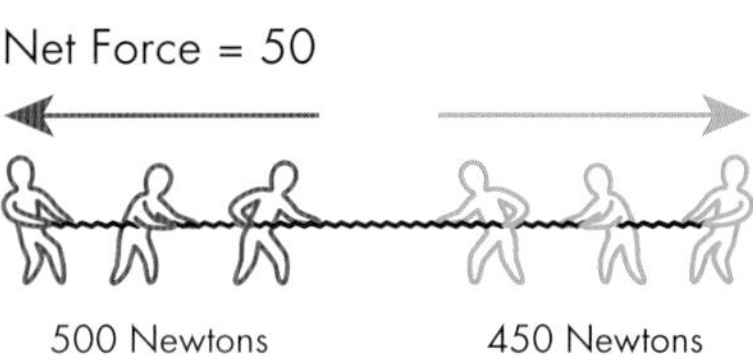

Neutral

1. An atom or particle that does not carry a charge.
2. A solution that has a pH of 7. Pure water is a neutral substance.

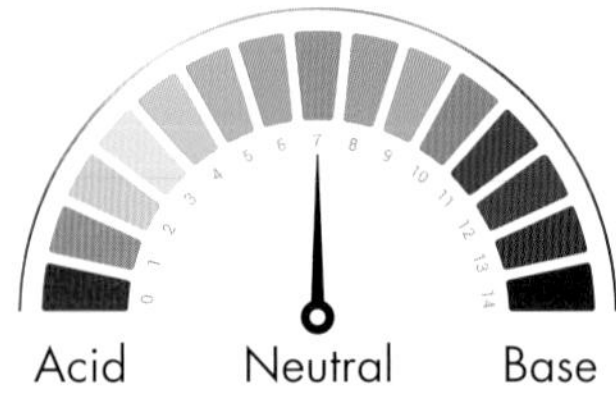

Neutron

A neutral particle found in the nucleus of the atom. It has an approximate mass of 1 unified atomic mass unit.

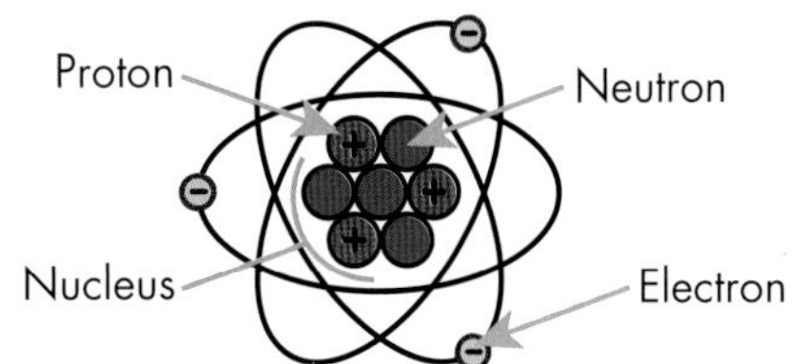

Calculating the Number of Neutrons in an Atom:

- ★ Find the atomic mass (found on the periodic table) of an atom; it is equal to the number of protons and neutrons together.
- ★ Calculate the number of neutrons by subtracting the number of protons (atomic number) from the atomic mass.

Example:
Lithium has an atomic mass of 6.9 or 7. Based on its atomic number, it has 3 protons. Lithium has 4 neutrons.

Newton's First Law of Motion

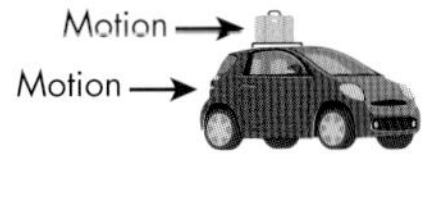

An object at rest will remain at rest unless acted upon by an outside force; an object will continue to travel in a straight line unless acted upon by an outside force. Also called the Law of Inertia.

Example:
When riding in a car, if the car suddenly stops, a rider not wearing a seat belt will continue moving at the speed of the car.

Newton's Laws of Motion

Three laws that show the relationships between forces acting on an object and the motion of the body.

Newton's Second Law of Motion

For an object to accelerate or move in the direction of the force placed upon it, you have to have enough force to overcome its mass.

Example:
The more mass in the car, the more force it will take to move it. The faster you want it to move, the more force you will need.

Newton's Third Law of Motion

For every action, there is an equal and opposite reaction.

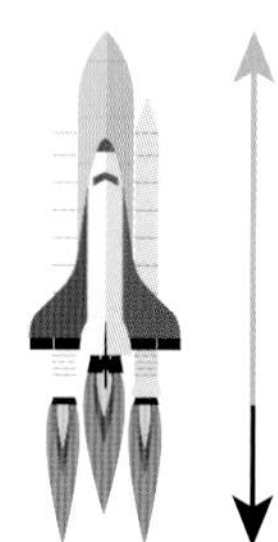

Example:
For a rocket to leave the ground, hot gasses have to push downward while the rocket moves up.

Nonmetals

Substances found on the right side of the periodic table. They generally are not good conductors of heat and energy, and most are gasses at room temperature.

Nuclear Energy

Energy created by the breaking (fission) or joining (fusion) of atomic nuclei (plural for nucleus).

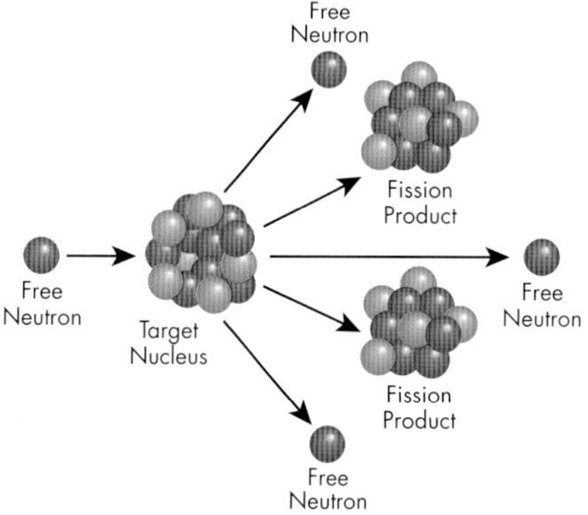

Nucleus

The central part of an atom that contains the protons and neutrons.

Parallel Circuit

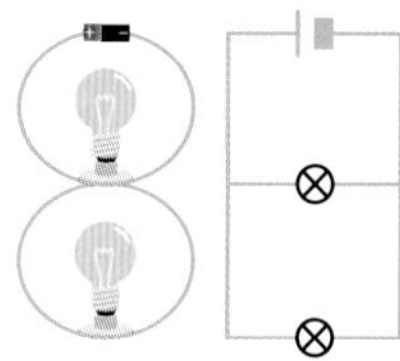

An electric circuit that has more than one path for the current to follow. If one light bulb (or resistor) is turned off or breaks, the current will follow the other path.

Particle

A very small piece or part of a substance or object.

Pendulum

An object suspended from a fixed point so it can swing (or oscillate) freely back and forth.

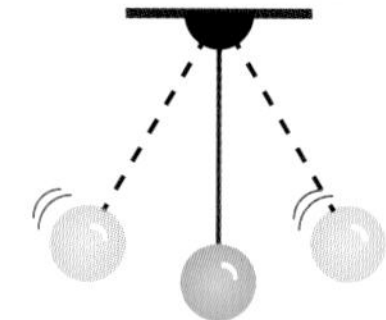

Calculating the Period of a Pendulum:

- ★ Using a stopwatch, measure the amount of time it takes for the pendulum to make one complete swing out and return to its starting point.

Period

1. A horizontal row on the periodic table.
2. Time needed for one complete swing out and back to a pendulum.

pH (Potential of Hydrogen)

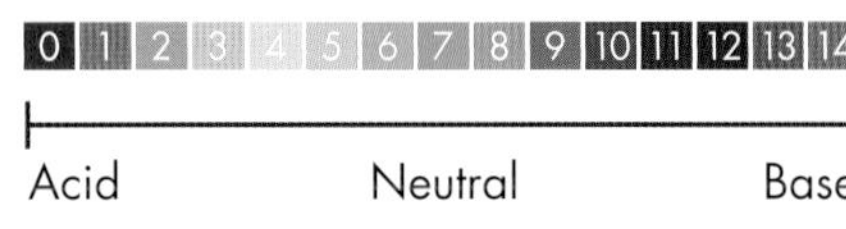

A measure of how acidic or basic a solution; 7 is considered neutral, while 1–6 are acidic and 8–14 are basic is. The further away from neutral, the stronger the acid or base. See page 140 for a list of common acids and bases.

Phase

Another term for state of matter. There are four phases of matter: solid, liquid, gas, and plasma.

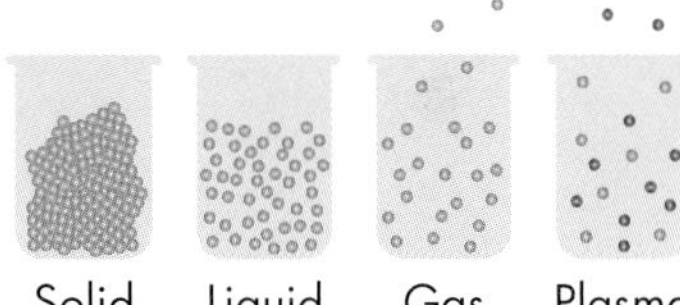

Physical Change

A change in size, shape, or state of matter that does not change a substance's composition.

Examples:
Water melting or freezing, crumpling a piece of paper, liquid evaporating, breaking glass

Physics

The study of matter, energy, and force.

Pitch

Low High

How high or low a sound is. It is determined by the frequency. The higher the frequency (number of waves in a second), the higher the pitch. The lower the frequency, the lower the pitch.

Plasma

1. A very hot, gas-like state of matter that occurs naturally on the sun and other stars. It also can be produced in fluorescent lights and plasma display televisions.
2. The liquid part of blood.

Potential Energy

Stored energy.

Potential Energy

Power

1. The rate at which work is done. Measured in watts.

Calculating Power (Work):

★ Use the formula: $P = \frac{W}{t}$

- P = power (watts)
- W = work (joules)
- t = time (seconds, minutes, hours)

2. The amount of electricity being used. Measured in watts.

Calculating Power (Electricity):

★ Use the formula: $P = V \bullet I$

- P = power (watts)
- V = voltage (volts)
- I = current (amps)

Product

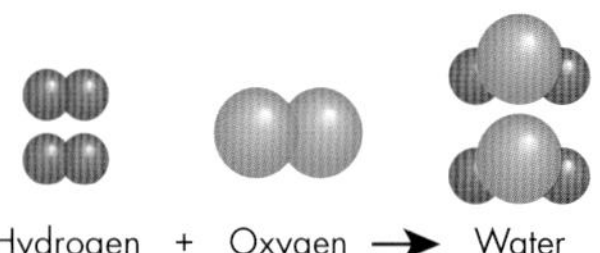

The substance or substances that are formed in a chemical reaction.

Property

Characteristics of an object or substance.

Examples:
Chemical properties (flammability), physical properties (density)

Protons

Positively charged particles that are located in the nucleus of the atom. They have an atomic mass of 1 u.

Calculating the Number of Protons in an Atom:

★ In an electrically stable atom, the element's atomic number equals the number of protons.

Example:
Hydrogen has an atomic number of 1, which means it has just one proton.

Pulley

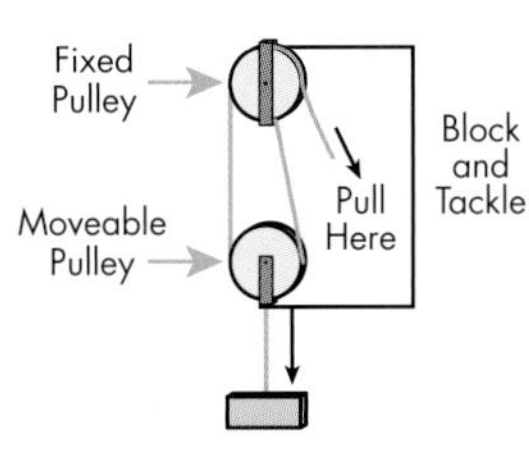

A simple machine made up of a grooved wheel that can turn freely in a frame called a block. There are two basic kinds: fixed (the pulley doesn't move) and moveable (the pulley moves along the rope). In addition, a block and tackle pulley is made of more than one pulley working together.

Radio Wave

A wave on the electromagnetic spectrum. It is the slowest with the longest wavelength.

Reactant

A substance that is participating in a chemical reaction.

Reflect (Reflection)

To throw or bend back light or sound when it hits a surface.

Examples:
Mirrors reflect light; echoes are reflected sound.

Refract (Refraction)

To bend light as it passes through a material or lens or from one state of matter to another.

Resistance

A measure of how much a material slows down or stops electricity. Measured in ohms.

Examples:
Rubber has higher resistance so it is a poor conductor of electricity. Copper has low resistance so it is a good conductor of electricity.

Calculating Resistance:

★ Use the formula: $R = \frac{V}{I}$

- R = resistance (ohms Ω)
- V = voltage (volts)
- I = current (amps)

Saturated Solution

A solution that has dissolved all of a substance that it is able to dissolve at a certain temperature.

Screw

An inclined plane wrapped around a cylinder core.

Examples:
Car jack, c-clamp, corkscrew

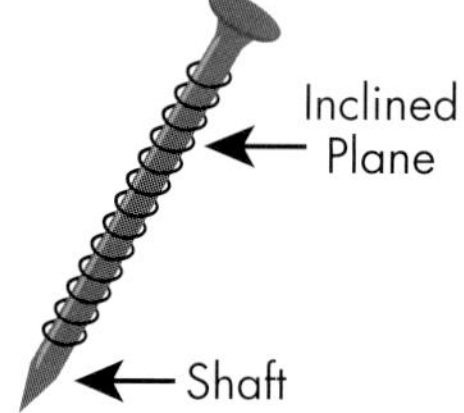

Series Circuit

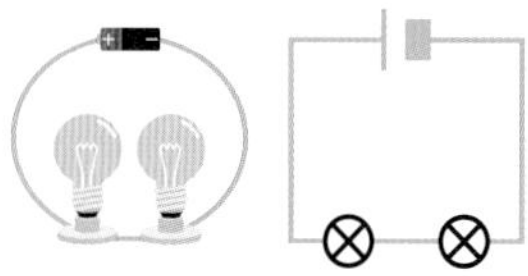

An electric circuit that has only one path for the current to follow. If one light bulb (or resistor) is turned off or breaks, the path is broken and the current will stop.

Simple Machine

A device without moving parts that is used to make work easier. There are six different kinds: lever, wheel and axle, pulley, wedge, inclined plane, and screw.

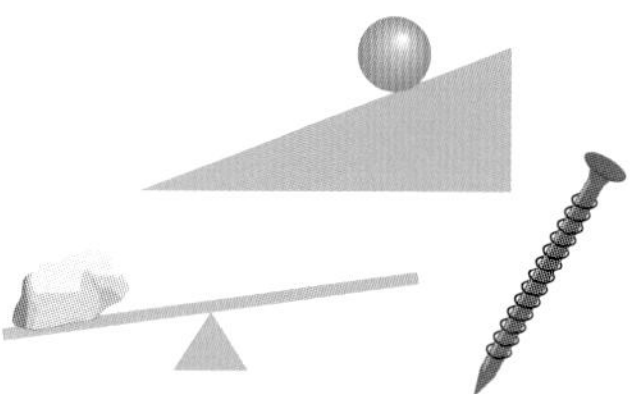

Solid

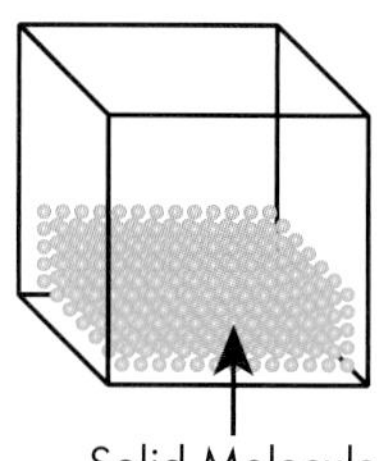

A state of matter with a definite shape and volume. Its particles have the lowest energy of all of the states of matter.

Solubility

The amount of substance or solute that can be dissolved in a certain amount of solvent.

Solubility Graph

A graph that shows the relationship between temperature and the amount of a certain solute that can be dissolved in water. See page 131 for more information.

Soluble

Able to be dissolved into another substance.

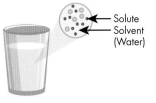

Solute
Solvent
(Water)

Solute

A substance that is being dissolved into something else.

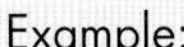

> Example:
> In making a powdered drink, the powder is the solute.

Solution

A homogeneous mixture of two or more substances; can be solids, gasses, or liquids.

> Example:
> Air (solution of various gasses), soda (solution of gas in a liquid), bronze (solid solution of copper and tin)

Solvent

The substance into which something is being dissolved.

> Example:
> In saltwater, the solvent is water.

Speed

The rate of motion of an object. It is represented by the distance over the time an object travels.

Calculating Speed:

★ Use the formula: $S = \frac{d}{t}$
- S = speed
- d = distance
- t = time

Static Electricity

Electricity caused by buildup of electrons on an object.

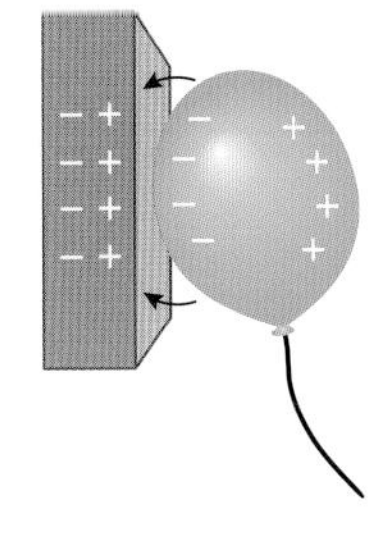

> Example:
> Rubbing a balloon against your hair and then placing it against a wall

Sublimation

When a solid turns into a gas.

Example:
Dry ice turns into carbon dioxide gas.

Supersaturated Solution

A solution that has more substance dissolved in it than it would normally be able to have dissolved at a certain temperature.

Example:
Heating and stirring water to dissolve sugar for sugar rock candy. If you just heated the water, it would not be able to dissolve as much as when it is stirred as well.

Temperature

Measure of the kinetic energy or motion of the molecules of a substance. It is expressed in Celsius, Fahrenheit, or Kelvin.

Calculating Celsius When Given Fahrenheit:

★ Use the formula: $°C = (5/9)(°F - 32)$

Calculating Fahrenheit When Given Celsius:

★ Use the formula: $°F = (1.8 \times °C) + 32$

Calculating Kelvin When Given Celsius:

★ Use the formula: $°K = °C + 273$

Terminal Velocity

The fastest speed an object can reach when falling.

Thermal Energy

A measure of the kinetic energy of a substance. As a substance heats up, its molecules have a higher kinetic energy and a higher thermal energy.

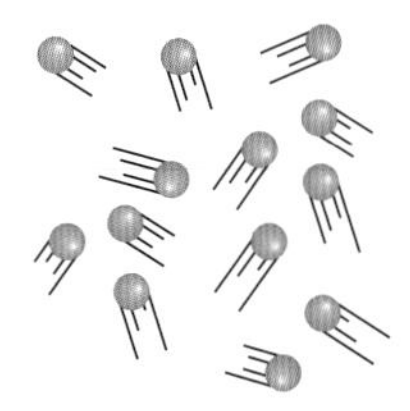

Low Thermal Energy
Low Temperature

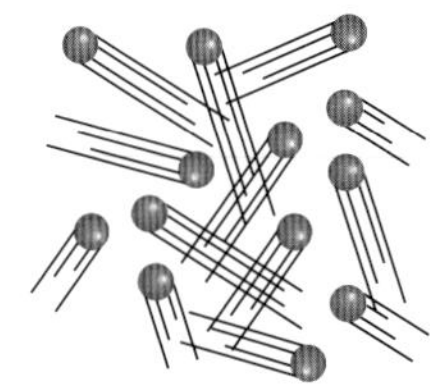

High Thermal Energy
High Temperature

PHYSICAL SCIENCES

Transverse Wave

A wave that travels at a 90° angle to the medium it is moving through.

Examples:
Water waves, light waves

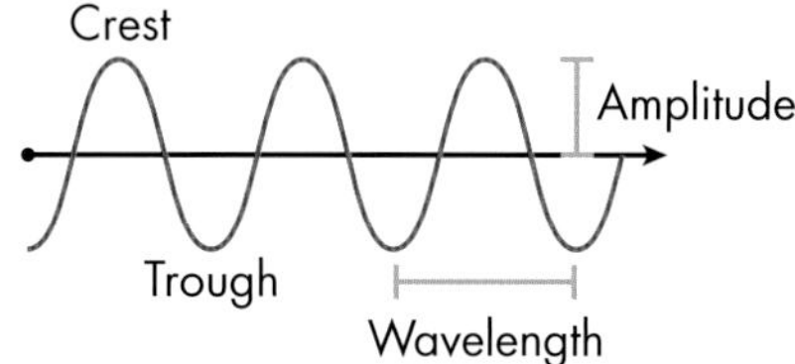

Trough

The lowest part of a transverse wave.

Ultraviolet Waves

A wave on the electromagnetic spectrum with a longer wavelength than x-rays but shorter than the visible spectrum.

Unsaturated Solution

A solution that can still have more of a certain substance dissolved in it.

Vacuum

A space without matter or air. Space is considered a vacuum.

Valence Electrons

The electrons located in the outermost electron shell of an atom. They are the electrons involved in chemical reactions.

Example:
Oxygen has two rings of electrons; the innermost one has two electrons. The second, or outermost, ring has six. These are the valence electrons. Oxygen has six valence electrons.

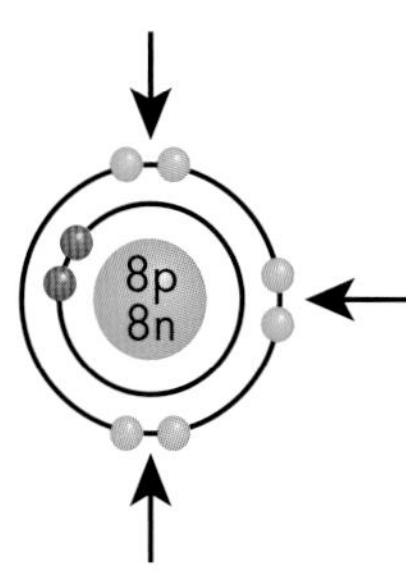

Vaporization

When a substance changes from liquid to gas. The process includes evaporation and boiling.

Velocity

The speed of an object in a certain direction.

Example:
If a car travels 100 km/hour from Houston to San Antonio and then travels 100 km/hour from San Antonio to Houston, its speed is the same, but its velocity is different.

Visible Spectrum

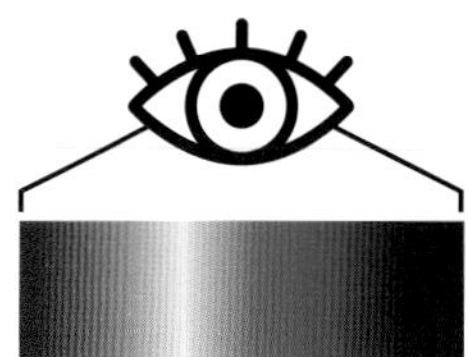

The part of the electromagnetic spectrum that can be seen (or is visible).

Voltage

The strength or force of the electrons or electrical current in a circuit. Technically, voltage is the difference of potential energy between two points of an electrical circuit. A good analogy is comparing electricity to water. High voltage is like water that is coming out of a power washer versus water that is coming out of a garden hose (lower voltage).

Example:
High voltage signs warn that the current traveling through the circuit has a lot of energy and strength and could be dangerous.

Calculating Voltage Using Resistance:

★ Use the formula: $V = IR$
- V = voltage (volts)
- I = current (amps)
- R = resistance (ohms Ω)

Calculating Voltage Using Power:

★ Use the formula: $V = \frac{P}{I}$
- V = voltage (volts)
- P = power (watts)
- I = current (amps)

Volume

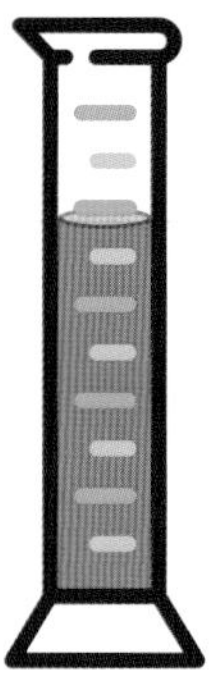

The amount of space an object occupies. Usually measured in L, ml, or cm^3 using a graduated cylinder.

Wave

The movement of energy (with or without matter).

Examples:
Light waves, electromagnetic waves, earthquake waves

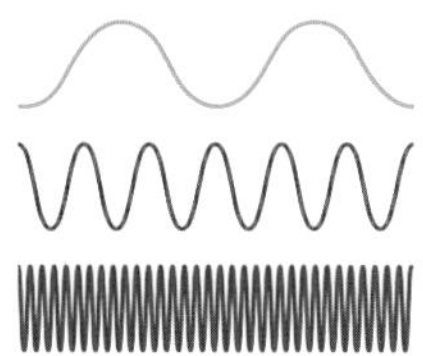

Wavelength

The distance between two crests or two troughs in a transverse wave or the length of one compression and one rarefaction in a compressional wave.

Calculating the Wavelength:

★ Use the formula: $\lambda = \frac{v}{F}$

- λ = wavelength (in meters)
- F = frequency (Hertz)
- v = speed (usually in m/sec)

Wedge

A simple machine with an inclined plane on one or both sides.

Examples:
Knife, axe, nail

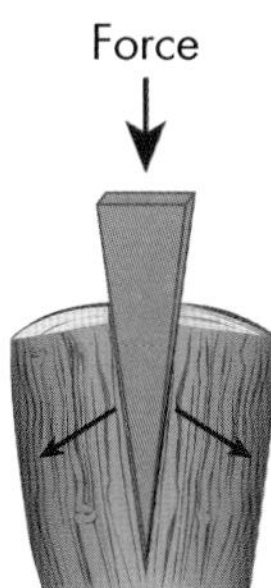

Weight

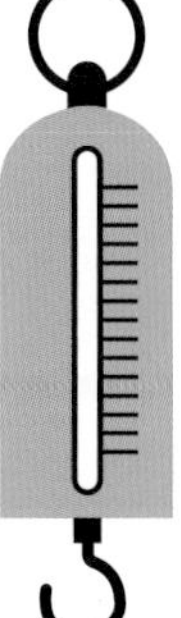

A measure of how much gravity pulls on an object. It is measured using a scale and is expressed in Newtons.

Wheel and Axle

A large wheel secured to a smaller wheel or shaft called an axle.

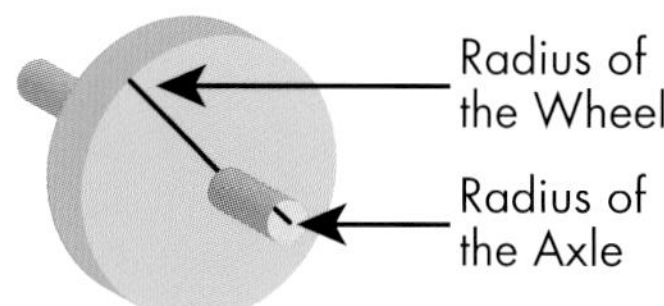

Examples:
Doorknob, screwdriver, steering wheel

Calculating the Mechanical Advantage of a Wheel and Axle:

- ★ Measure the radius of the wheel and divide by the radius of the axle.

Work

A force acting through a distance.

Calculating Work:

- ★ Use the formula: W = F • d
  - W = work (joules)
  - F = force (Newtons)
  - d = distance (meters)

X-Ray

A wave found on the electromagnetic spectrum. Its wavelength is longer than gamma rays but shorter than ultraviolet waves.

EARTH SCIENCES

Abrasion

The process of the wearing away of rock by particles carried by wind, water, or ice.

Example:
Rocks in the bottom of a glacier rub or scrape the bedrock as the glacier moves over it.

Absolute Dating

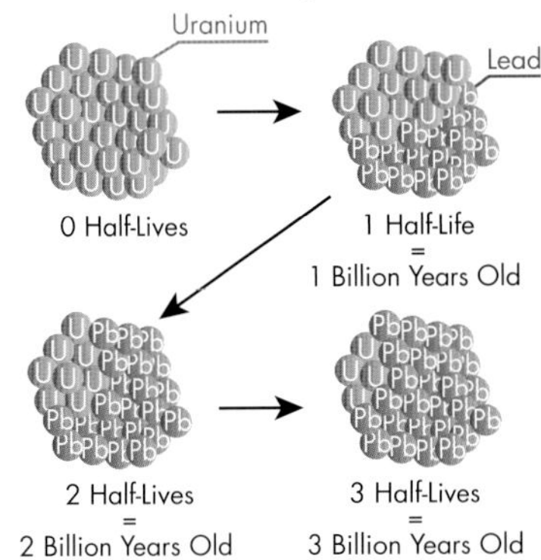

A process that provides an approximate age in years when determining the age of a fossil. It is sometimes called radioactive dating because the dating requires calculating radioactive half-lives.

Asthenosphere

A relatively thin layer of the Earth, located in the upper part of the mantle, on which the Earth's plates rest and move.

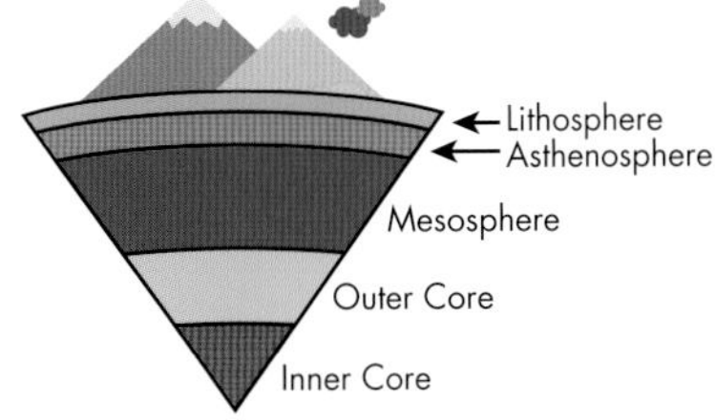

Atmosphere

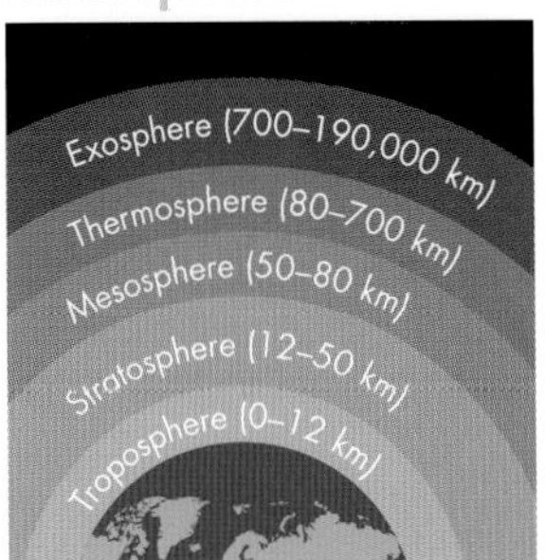

The layers of gasses that surround the Earth (or other planets).

Biomass

Plant material, animal waste, or vegetation that is used as a fuel or energy source.

Examples:
Wood, manure, yard clippings

Biosphere

The part of the Earth and its atmosphere that supports life.

Cementation

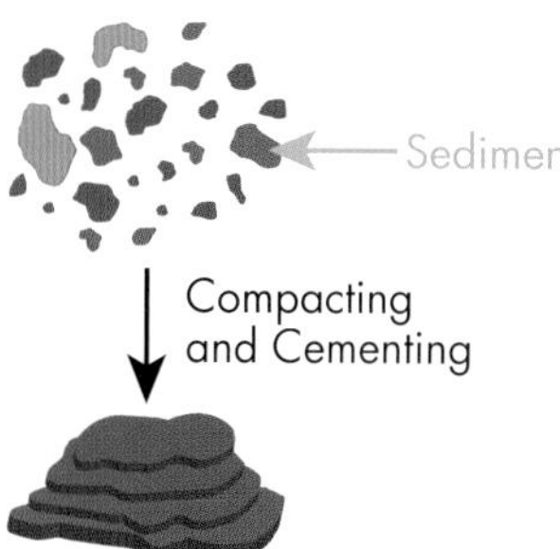

The last step in the formation of some sedimentary rocks. Minerals seep into the cracks between the sediments and cement them together.

Chemical Weathering

A form of weathering in which rocks and minerals are transformed into new substances.

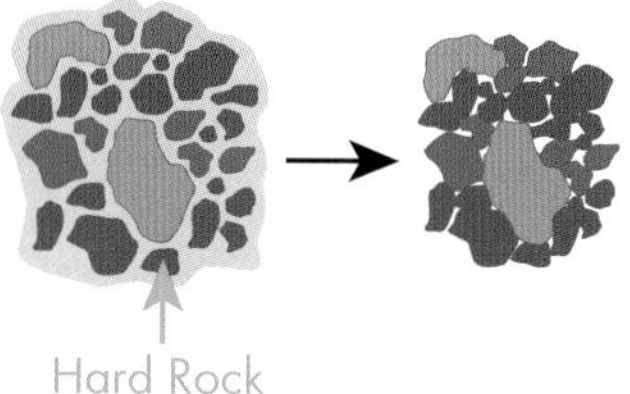

Example:
Rainwater hits a hard rock that has areas of softer rock in it. The acid in the rain interacts with the soft areas of the rock, and it breaks apart.

Cirrus

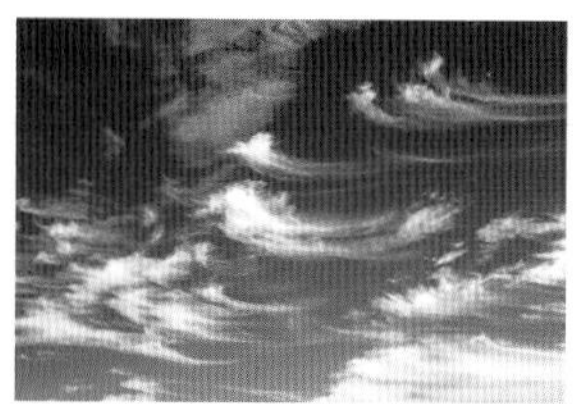

A high-altitude cloud with a thin white and wispy appearance.

Cleavage

A line or plane that a rock will break along naturally.

Cold Front

A weather front created when a cold air mass replaces a warm air mass. Associated with thunderstorms and cooler weather.

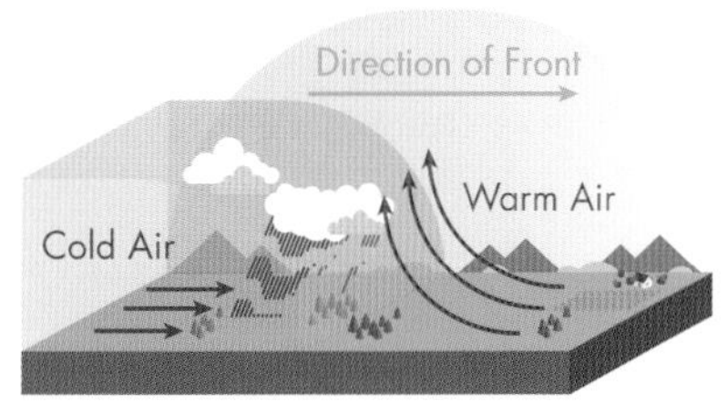

Compaction

The compressing of rock and sediments that can form sedimentary rocks.

Condensation

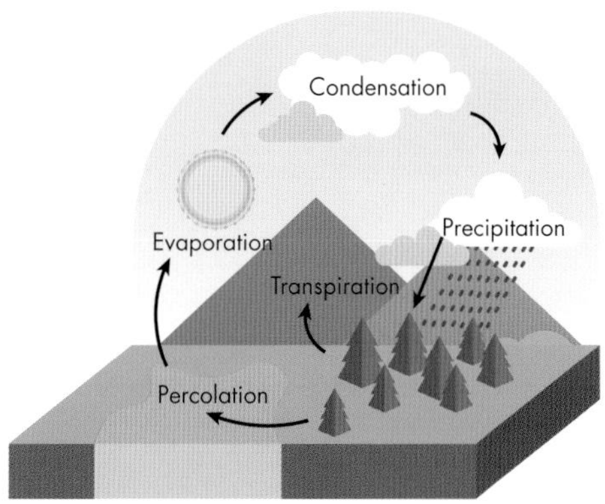

When water vapor changes into liquid. In the water cycle, this step leads to precipitation.

Conduction

The transfer of heat or electricity by direct contact.

Example:
The handle of a metal spoon gets hot when the spoon is left in a pot of boiling water.

Continental Drift

225 Million Years Ago

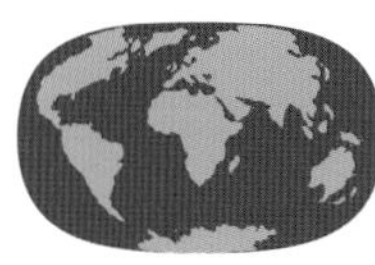

Present Day

The theory that the continents can move and drift freely on the surface of the Earth; usually credited to Alfred Wegener.

Convection

A heat transfer through liquids and gasses. Also known as convection currents.

Convergent Boundary

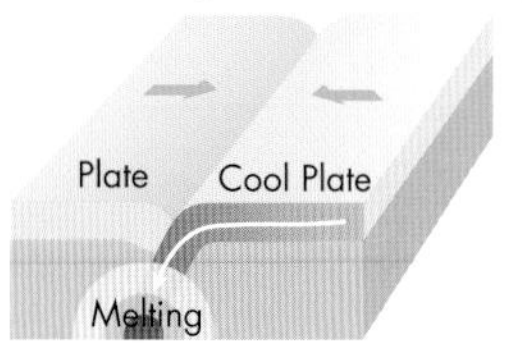

A place where two or more plates come together.

Core

The innermost part of the Earth. It is composed of an iron and nickel liquid outer core and a solid iron inner core.

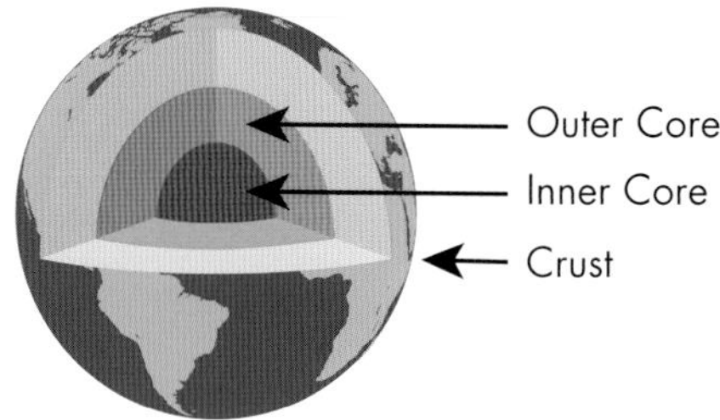

Crust

The outermost layer of the Earth's surface. It is broken into large pieces called plates, ranging from approximately 3 miles (5 km) to 47 miles (75 km) in thickness.

Cumulus

A dense, fluffy white cloud with a flat base and rounded top.

Delta

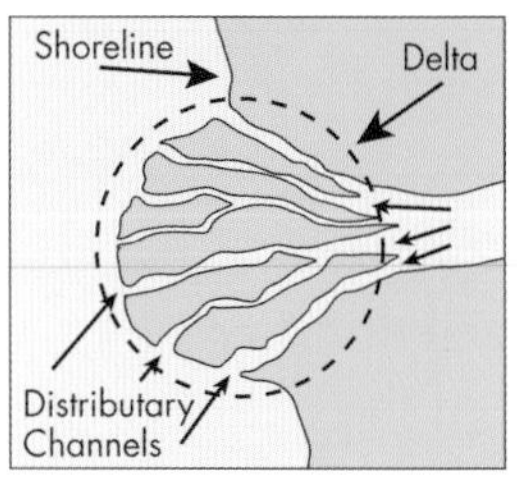

A fan-shaped landform formed at the mouth of a river as the river slows down and sediments are deposited.

Deposition

The dropping of material that has been picked up and transported by wind, water, or ice.

Dew Point

The temperature at which water vapor begins to condense out of the air and forms dew.

Divergent Boundary

A boundary in which two plates are moving away from each other.

Example:
The Mid-Atlantic Ridge found in the center of the Atlantic Ocean

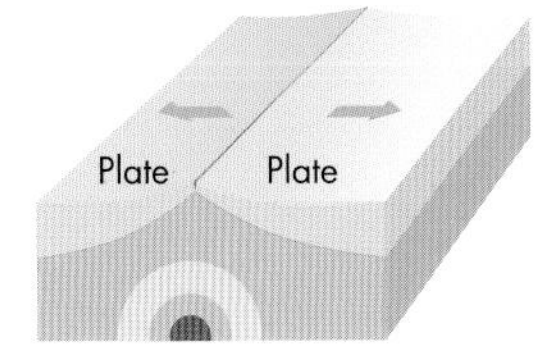

El Niño

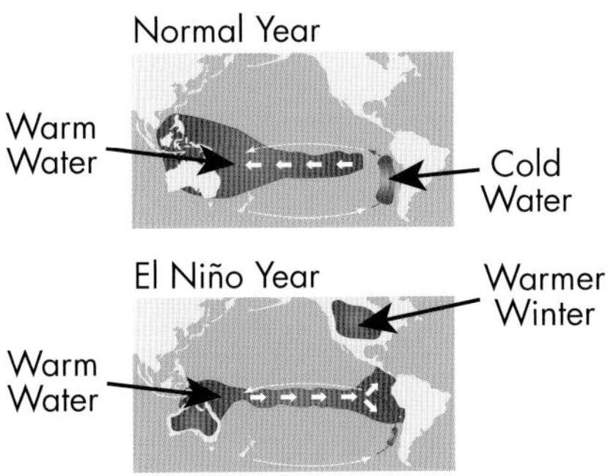

A weather pattern that occurs in the Pacific Ocean when winds cause warm water from the equator to move to the east toward Central and South America. This warm water means more storms could occur in these areas.

Eon	Era	Period	Epoch
Phanerozoic	Cenozoic	Neogene	
		Paleogene	
	Mesozoic	Cretaceous	
		Jurassic	
		Triassic	
	Paleozoic	Permian	
		Carboniferous: Pennsylvanian, Mississippian	
		Devonian	
		Silurian	
		Ordovician	
		Cambrian	

Eon

A period of geological time that equals one billion years.

Epicenter

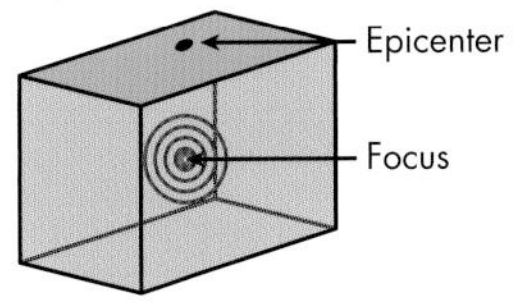

The point on the Earth's surface that is directly above the focus of an earthquake.

Epoch

A period of geological time that is divided into ages. See *Eon*.

EQ–EX

Equinox

The date when the sun crosses the equator, so day and night are approximately the same length. Occurs around March 20 and September 22.

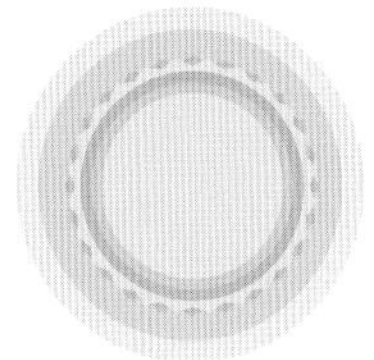

Era

The longest division of geologic time. See *Eon*.

Examples:
Precambrian, Paleozoic, Mesozoic, Cenozoic

Erosion

The process of moving soil and rock by water, wind, or glacial action.

Evaporation

The process in the water cycle in which water from the oceans and lakes is heated up enough by the sun to turn into water vapor in the atmosphere. See *Condensation*.

Exosphere

The uppermost region of the Earth's atmosphere; where the atmosphere mixes with space. See *Atmosphere*.

Extrusive

Igneous rocks that are formed from lava above the Earth's surface. Usually have very small or no crystals.

Examples:
Pumice, obsidian, basalt

Fault (Fault Line)

A crack or fracture in the Earth's crust along which movement occurs. There are three main types: normal fault (the hanging wall slips down), reverse fault (the hanging wall is pushed up), and strike-slip (the pieces of crust move past one another).

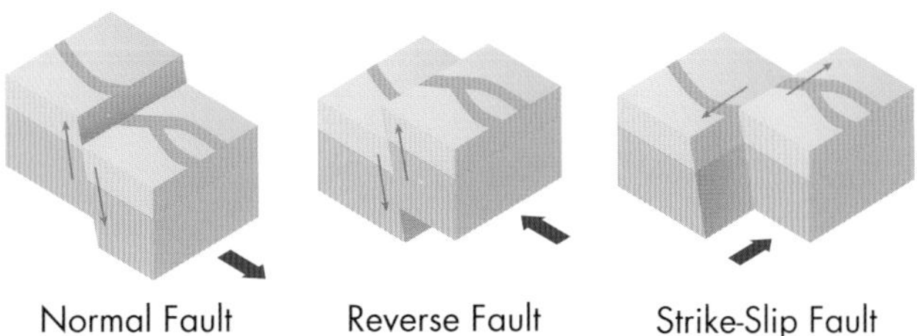

Fission

A nuclear reaction in which an atomic nucleus is split into fragments, releasing a significant amount of energy.

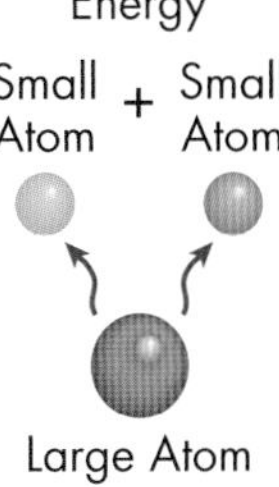

Focus

The exact location where the crust moved, causing an earthquake. See *Epicenter*.

Fold

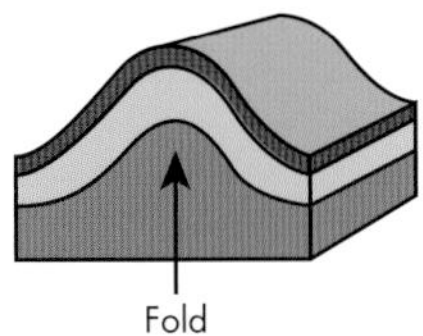

A bend in the layers of rock.

Foliated

A rock that has a layered appearance. This is usually associated with metamorphic rocks.

Fossil

The remains or impression of a once living organism.

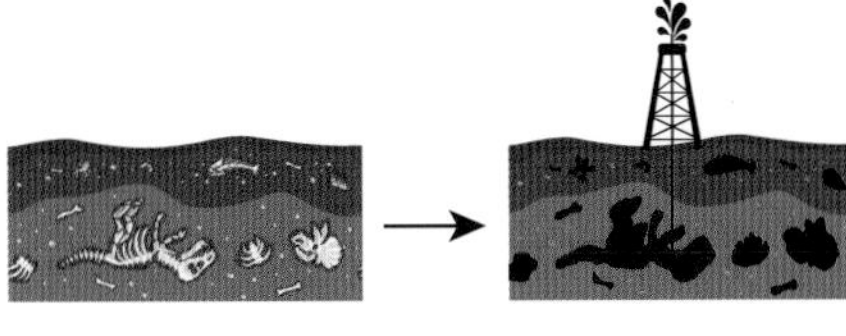

Fossil Fuel

A natural fuel, usually coal or natural gas, created from the remains of living things.

FU–GR

Fusion

A nuclear reaction in which smaller atomic nuclei are brought together to form a larger nucleus, releasing energy. This occurs naturally in stars and our sun.

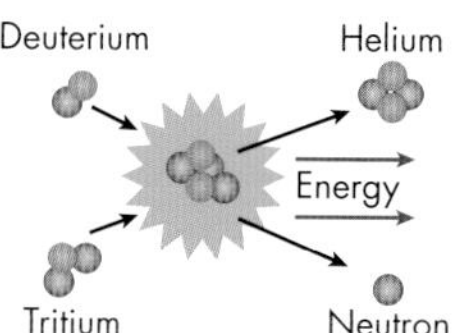

Generator

A machine that converts mechanical energy (energy in motion) to electrical energy.

Geothermal (Hydrothermal) Energy

Using the heat from within the Earth to create energy. Hydrothermal energy is specifically using the hot steam in the Earth's crust.

Glacier

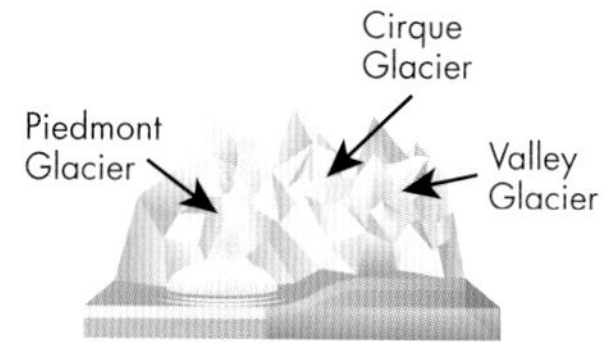

A large river of ice slowly flowing over a landmass as its mass and gravity force it forward. Although it stays year-round, it will move forward or recede based on the snowfall and temperatures.

Greenhouse Effect

When the heat from the sun is trapped in the lower layers of the Earth's atmosphere, making the average temperatures warmer.

Groundwater

Water that is found beneath Earth's surface. Groundwater is stored in permeable (filled with small holes) rock called aquifers.

Half-Life

The amount of time it takes for half of a radioactive material to decay.

Amount of Time Passed	Percentage of Original Amount That Is Still Present
0 half-lives	100%
1 half-life	50%
2 half-lives	25%
3 half-lives	12.5%
4 half-lives	6.25%
5 half-lives	3.125%
6 half-lives	1.5625%

Humidity

A measure of the amount of water vapor in the air. Expressed in a percent using a hygrometer.

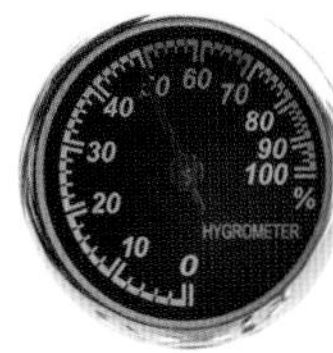

Humus

The organic part of soil. Usually dark in color, it is created by the decomposition of living material.

Hydroelectricity

Electricity that is created by running water.

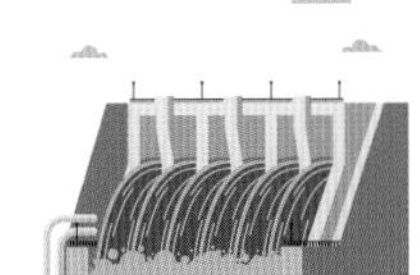

Igneous Rock

A rock formed from molten material, either at or below the Earth's surface. See *Rock Cycle*.

Examples:
Pumice, basalt, granite, obsidian

Inexhaustible Resource

A natural resource that will not be exhausted or consumed completely.

Examples:
Solar energy, wind energy

Intrusive

Igneous rocks that are formed from magma below the Earth's surface. Usually have larger crystals. See *Extrusive*.

Examples:
Granite, diorite, gabbro

La Niña

A weather pattern that occurs in the Pacific Ocean when winds cause warm water from the equator to move to the west toward Australia and up into Asia. This movement causes cold water to rise near South America, impacting weather along the west side of South, Central, and North America.

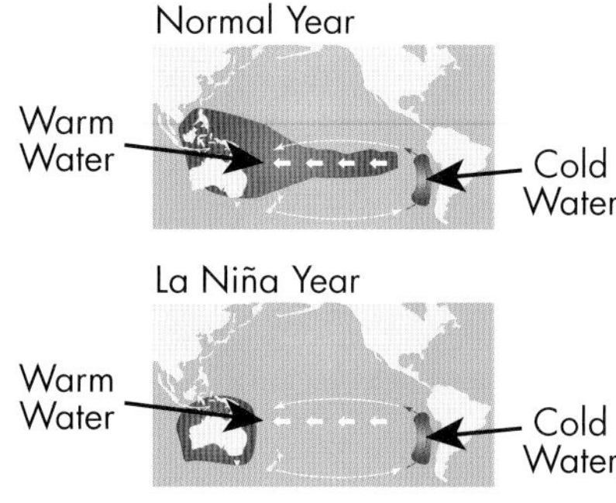

Latitude

A measurement that tells location based on how far north or south of the equator.

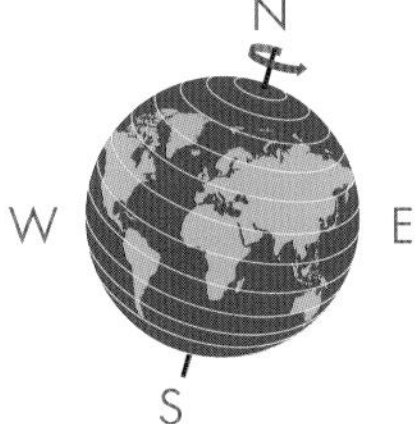

Lava

Molten rock at or above the Earth's surface.

Lithosphere

The strong outer layer of the Earth that is divided into 12 major plates and many more small ones. See *Plate Tectonics*.

Longitude

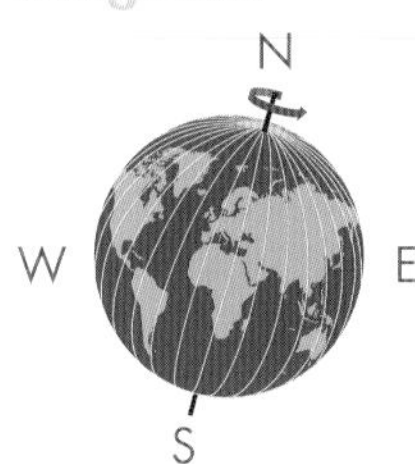

A measurement that tells location based on how far east or west of the prime meridian.

Luster

A description of the surface of a crystal, rock, or mineral.

Examples:
Metallic, nonmetallic, dull

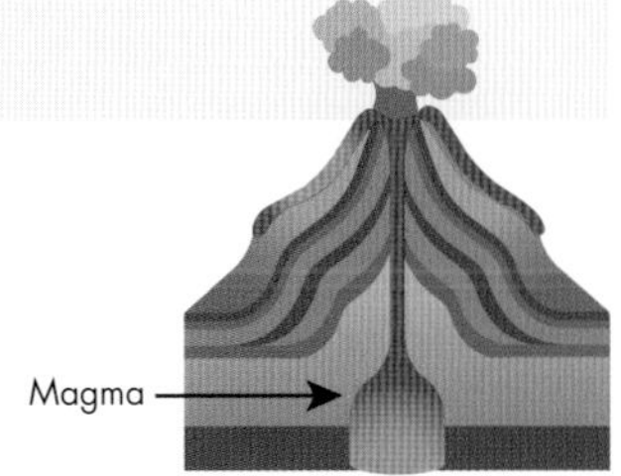

Magma

Molten rock below the Earth's surface; contains dissolved gasses.

Mantle

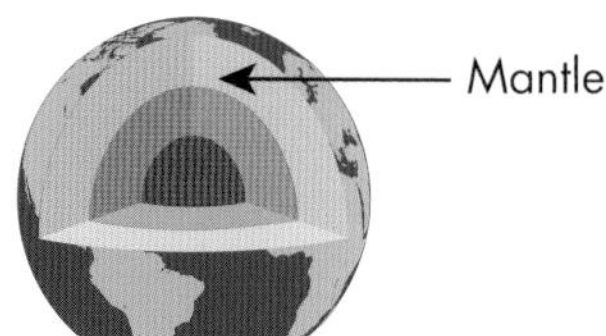

The middle layer of the Earth. Although considered solid, it can move. Comprises most of the Earth's mass.

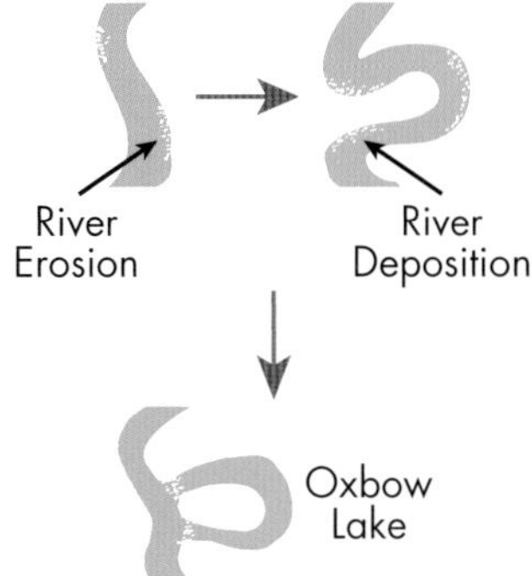

Meander

A bend in a river formed by erosion and deposition along its banks. It can eventually be cut off and turn into an oxbow lake.

Mechanical Weathering

See *Physical Weathering*.

Mesosphere

The middle layer of the Earth's atmosphere. Temperatures decrease in this layer as altitude is increased. See *Atmosphere*.

Metamorphic Rock

A rock formed by heat and pressure deep within the Earth's crust. See *Rock Cycle*.

Examples:
Slate, gneiss, marble

ME–OR

Meteorologist

A scientist who predicts and reports weather conditions.

Mineral

A naturally occurring solid that has a definite chemical composition, color, hardness, and crystalline structure.

Examples:
Diamond, quartz, gold, silver

Moraine

An accumulation of the sediments left behind by a glacier.

Nonrenewable Resource

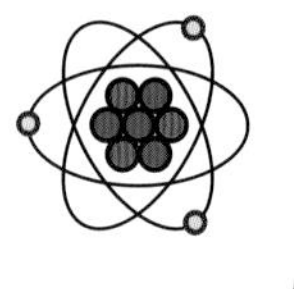

A natural resource that cannot be restored after use or is being used at such a rate that it cannot be replaced as quickly as it is being consumed.

Examples:
Oil, natural gas, petroleum

Nuclear Power

Power created by splitting radioactive nuclei (plural of nucleus).

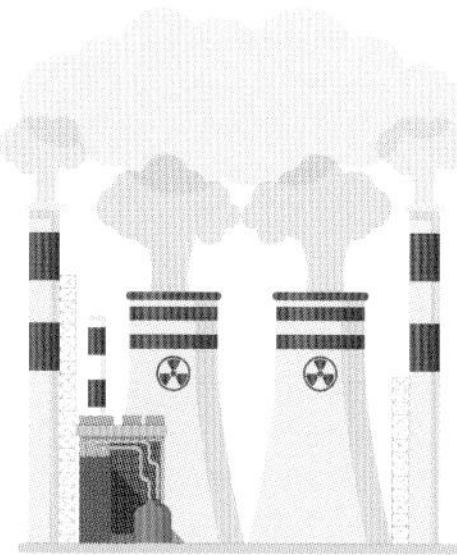

Ore

A mineral that can be mined for profit.

Examples:
Aluminum, iron, copper

Oxidation

The chemical name for rusting. When a metal object rusts, it is reacting (or oxidizing) with the oxygen in the atmosphere.

Ozone

A gas found in the ozone layer of the atmosphere. Its chemical formula is O_3 and it helps reflect the harmful rays of the sun back into space.

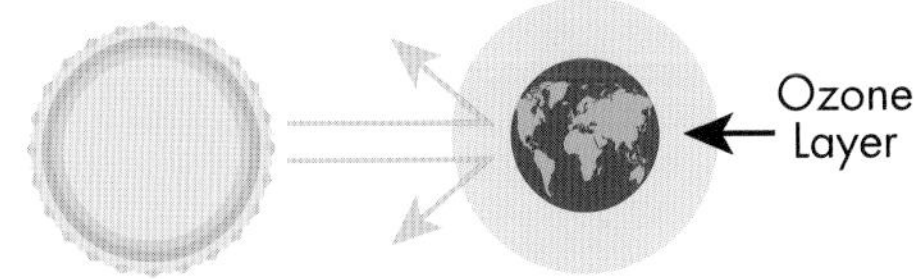

Pangaea

The name of a supercontinent that is believed to have existed before the continents drifted apart. Proposed by Alfred Wegener as part of the theory of continental drift.

Percolation

When water slowly passes through the ground to become groundwater.

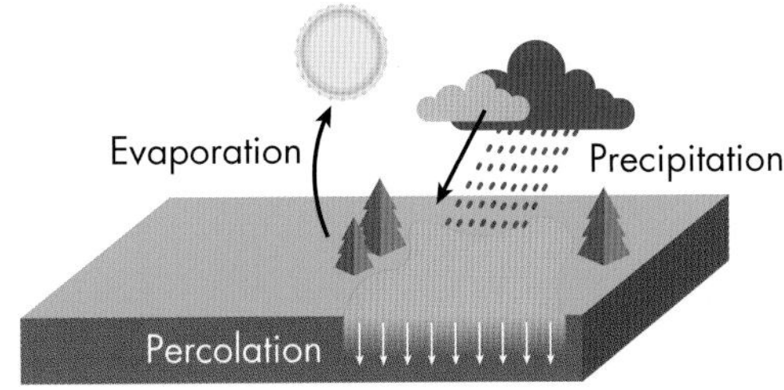

Period

The division of geologic time into which eras are divided. See *Eon*.

> Examples:
> The Mesozoic Era is divided into the Cretaceous, Jurassic, and Triassic periods.

Permeability

The ability of a material to transmit fluids. An aquifer must have permeable rock for the water to move through it.

Physical Weathering

The process of breaking down rocks into smaller fragments using physical means.

Example:
Ice wedging (water gets into cracks in rocks and freezes, breaking the rock apart)

Plate Tectonics

The theory that the crust of the Earth is broken into large pieces called plates that are being pushed and moved through convection currents in the Earth's mantle.

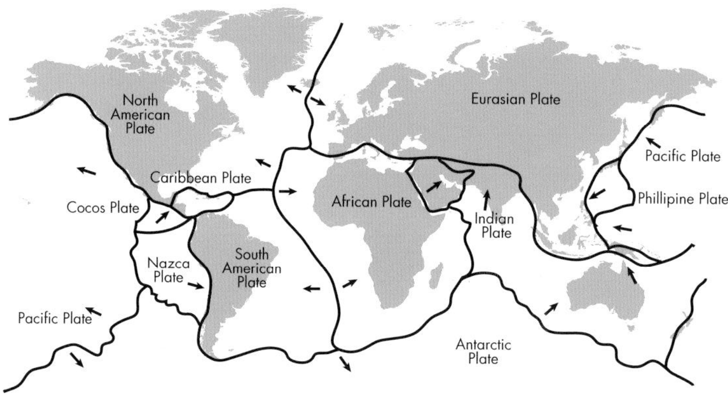

Precipitation

Any form of water that falls to the Earth's surface. See *Water Cycle*.

Examples:
Rain, snow, sleet, hail

Principle of Superposition

Used in relative dating. It states that the deepest rock layers are the oldest.

Radiation

A transfer of energy that does not require matter to take place.

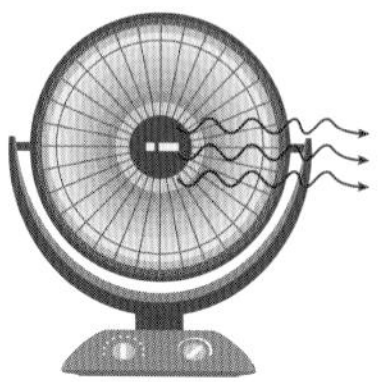

Examples:
Sunlight, heat lamps

Relative Dating

Determining the age of rock layers relative to the other rock layers.

Example:
If a fossil is found in an upper layer, it is younger than the fossils found below it.

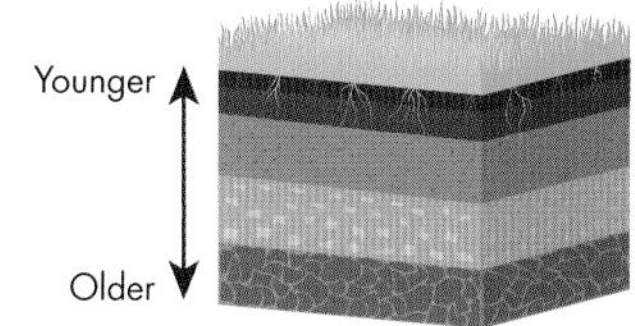

Renewable Resource

A natural resource that can be replenished at the current rate it is being consumed by humans.

Examples:
Fresh water, wood, biomass, geothermal power

Richter Scale

A scale used to measure the strength (magnitude) of an earthquake. An increase of each number on the scale equals an increase of 10 times the number before it.

Example:
A two on the Richter scale is 10 times stronger than a one on the Richter scale.

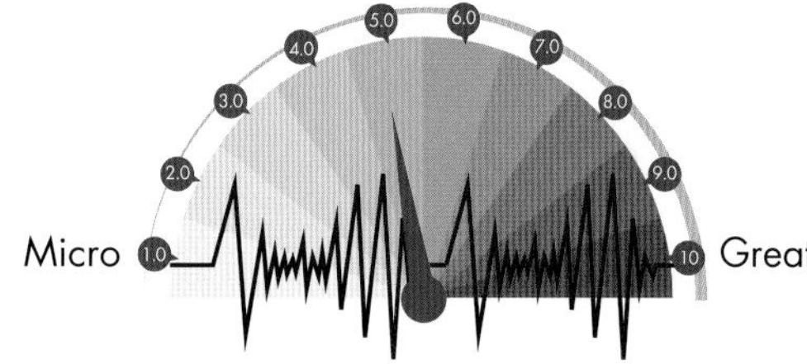

Rock Cycle

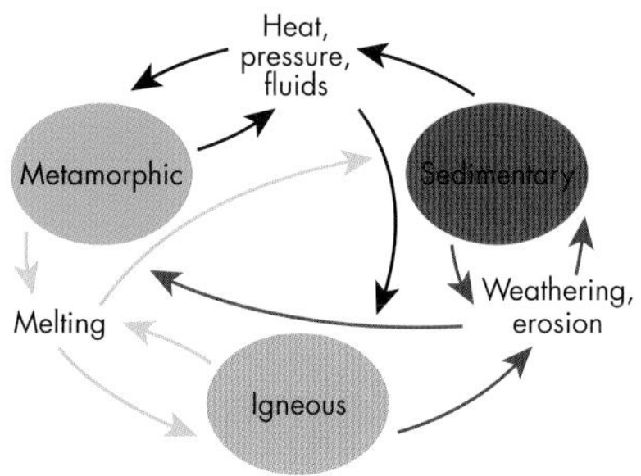

The sequence of events that shows how rocks initially form and change over time.

Runoff

Water that is not absorbed by rocks or soil so it flows over the ground. See *Water Cycle*.

Seafloor Spreading

Occurs on the floor of the Atlantic Ocean at the mid-ocean ridge. When magma comes up from the mantle through the Mid-Atlantic Ridge, it hardens. As it goes from liquid to solid, its volume expands. This expansion is slowly causing the seafloor of the Atlantic Ocean to expand or spread.

Season

Changes caused by the 23.5° tilt of the Earth's axis toward or away from the sun.

Sedimentary Rock

A rock formed by the compaction or cementation of layers of sediment being laid down on top of each other. See *Rock Cycle*.

Examples:
Coal, limestone, conglomerate, shale

Sediments

Weathered materials carried and deposited by wind, water, or ice. See *Rock Cycle*.

Seismic Wave

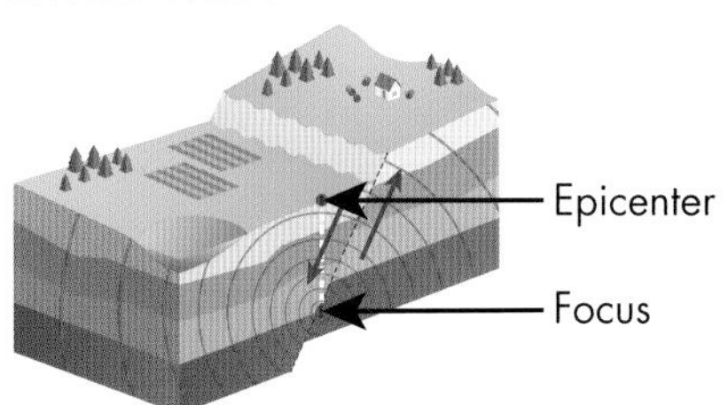

A wave that is caused by a sudden movement in the Earth's crust.

Seismograph

An instrument that detects and records the intensity, direction, and duration of an earthquake.

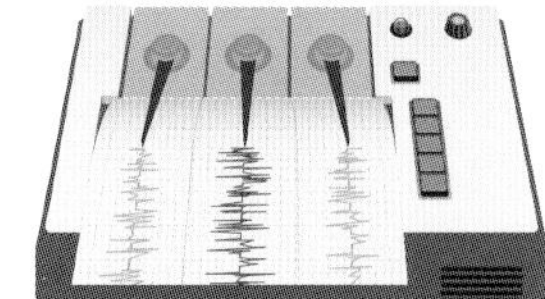

Solar Power

An inexhaustible energy source in which the energy of the sun is captured and converted into useful types of energy. The energy usually is captured with large solar panels located in direct sunlight.

Solstice

When the sun is at its northernmost point of the year, or the southernmost point of the year. The summer solstice, June 21, is the longest day, most light hours, of the year. December 21, the winter solstice is the shortest day, least daylight hours, of the year.

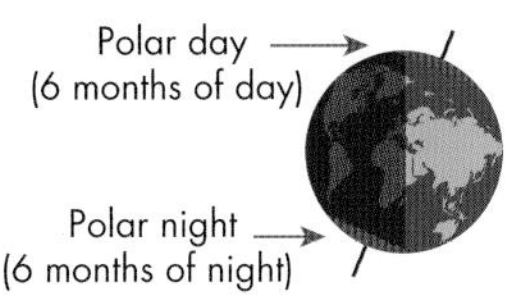

Summer Solstice
(June 21)

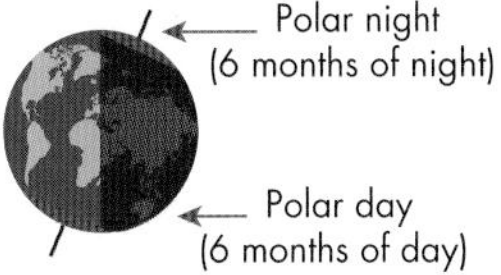

Winter Solstice
(December 21)

Stationary Front

When air masses meet each other, but neither is strong enough to move the other. This front may cause clouds and fog, as well as rain. See *Weather Map Symbols*.

Stratosphere

The layer of the atmosphere immediately above the troposphere. It contains the ozone layer. See *Atmosphere*.

Stratus

A grey cloud with layers that is close to the ground.

Example:
Fog

ST–TR

Streak

The color of the powder left behind when a mineral is rubbed against a hard surface (usually a streak plate).

Subduction Zone

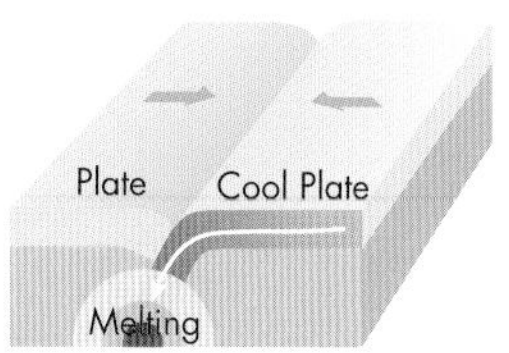

An area where one edge of a crustal plate is forced below another plate; associated with a convergent plate boundary.

Thermosphere

The layer of the Earth's atmosphere directly beneath the exosphere. Temperatures increase in this layer as altitude increases. See *Atmosphere*.

Tidal Power

Energy created by ocean waves that is captured and used to turn a turbine.

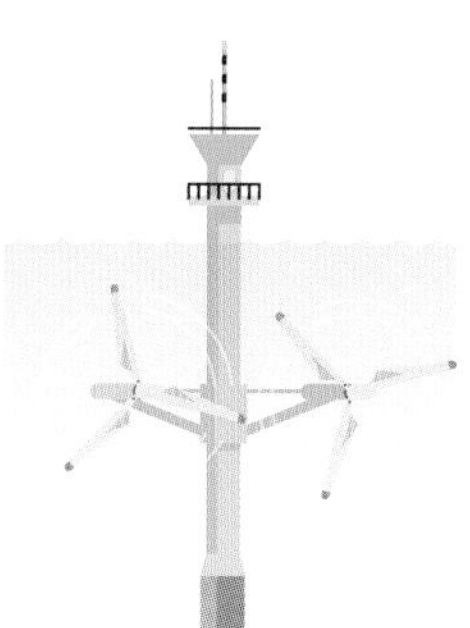

Topographic Map

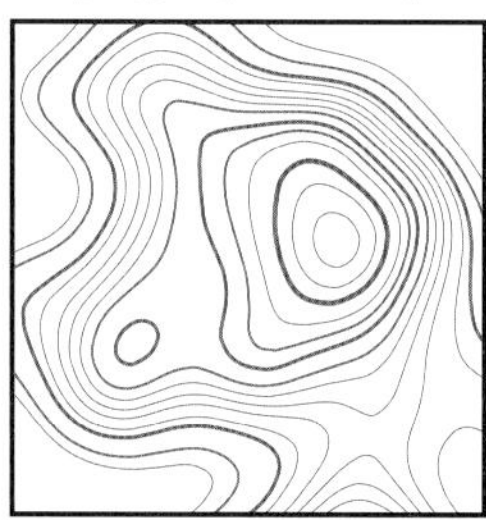

A map that is a two-dimensional representation of a three-dimensional land surface. These maps show the size, shape, and elevation of various land features.

Trace Fossil

A fossil that shows that an animal was once there, without being a part of the animal itself. It could be a footprint, trail, or animal home.

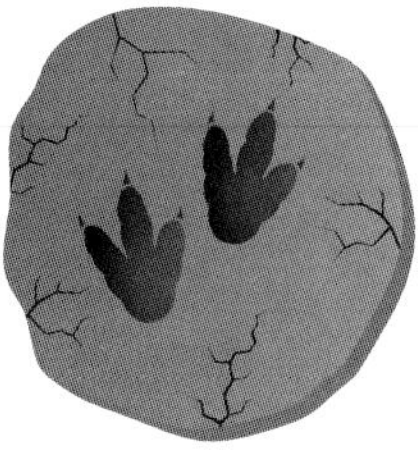

Transform Boundary

A boundary in which two plates are passing beside each other.

Example:
San Andreas Fault

Troposphere

The layer of the atmosphere that is closest to the surface of the Earth. Clouds and weather are found in this layer. See *Atmosphere*.

Tsunami

A huge wave that is caused when the waves from an underwater earthquake travel through the water. As the waves get closer to shore, they begin to pile up until they smash on shore.

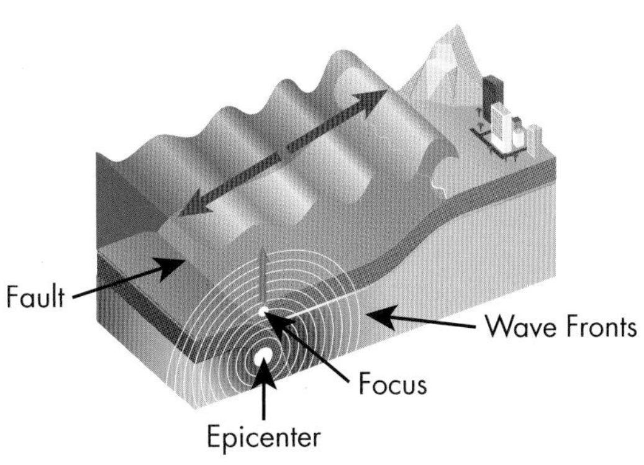

Warm Front

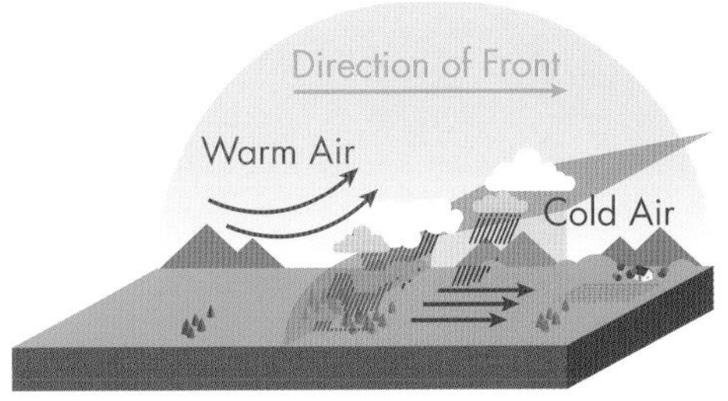

A weather front created when a warm air mass replaces a cold air mass. Associated with rainstorms and warmer weather.

Water Cycle

The cycle that shows how water is transferred and changed from the bodies of water into the atmosphere and then back to the ocean.

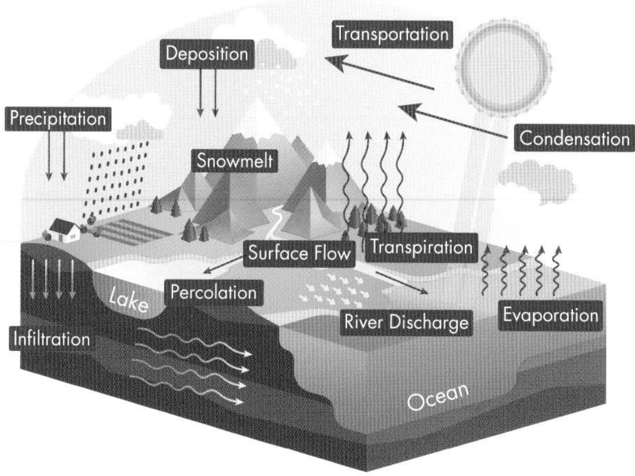

Weather Map Symbols

Symbols or letters used on a weather map to show the current weather. A complete list is included in the quick reference guide on page 143.

Common Symbols:

Weathering

The process of breaking down rock into smaller pieces and sediments. There are two types: physical and chemical.

Wind Power

A renewable energy source in which the energy of wind is captured and converted into useful types of energy. Usually captured with large wind turbines located in areas of constant wind.

SPACE SCIENCES

Asteroid

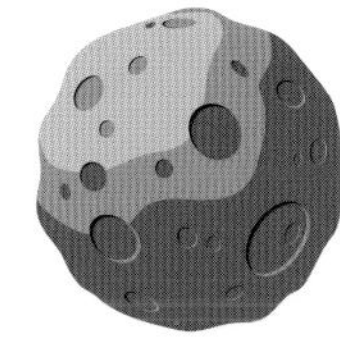

Any of the rocks or bodies in space that revolve around the sun, usually located between Mars and Jupiter.

Black Dwarf

The final stage in the life cycle of a main sequence star. When it reaches this stage, the star has compressed in on itself to a very small volume. It no longer produces energy. It no longer shines.

Black Hole

An area in space with such strong gravitational pull that even light cannot escape its pull.

Comet

A body in space that travels in a long orbit around the sun. It is made up a solid head with a long vapor tail that always points away from the sun.

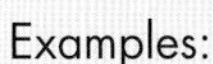

Examples:
Halley's Comet (appears every 76 years) and
Hale-Bopp (appears every 2,400 years)

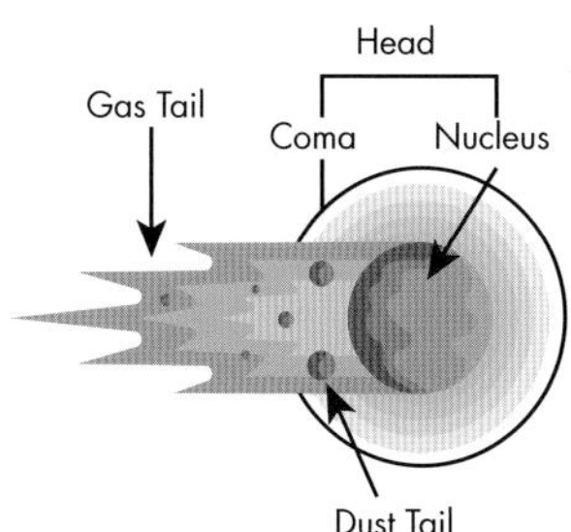

Constellation

A formation of stars that seem to form pictures in the night sky.

Examples:
Cassiopeia, Orion, Cygnus, the astrological signs

Corona

The plasma-like atmosphere of the sun. It is what is visible during a total solar eclipse.

Crescent

Waning Crescent

Waxing Crescent

One of the phases of the moon, associated with the coming (waxing) or going (waning) of the new moon.

Eclipse

When a body in space is either partially or completely blocked from sight.

Lunar

- ★ Occurs when the Earth's shadow falls on the moon, blocking it from sight. Occurs about every 6 months.

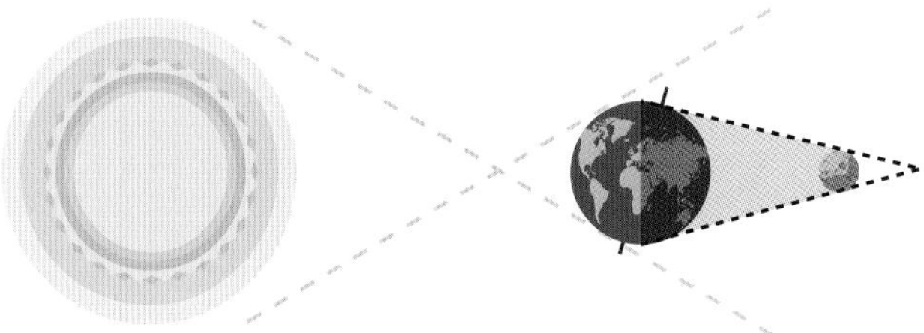

Solar

- ★ Occurs when the moon passes directly between the Earth and sun, so the sun is blocked from view. Usually lasts less than 8 minutes.

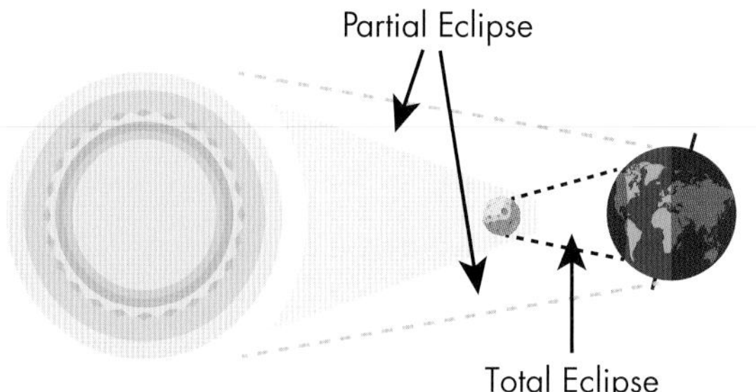

Elliptical Galaxy

A galaxy with no spiral structure that seems to have an elliptical shape, containing mostly older stars.

Examples:
Messier 32, Messier 87, Leo I

Full Moon

The phase of the moon when it is directly behind the Earth and completely lit by the sun's light.

Galaxy

A large group of stars, dust, gas, and other bodies held together by gravity. They are classified by their shapes. There are three main types: elliptical, spiral, and irregular.

Elliptical

Spiral

Irregular

Gibbous

The moon's phases in which more than half of the moon's surface is visible.

Inner Planets

The rocky planets in our solar system, closest to the sun. They include Mercury, Venus, Earth, and Mars.

Irregular Galaxy

A galaxy that has a unique shape and is not symmetrical. Comprised of both young and older stars, it is the least common shape for galaxies.

Examples:
Large Magellanic Cloud, Messier objects

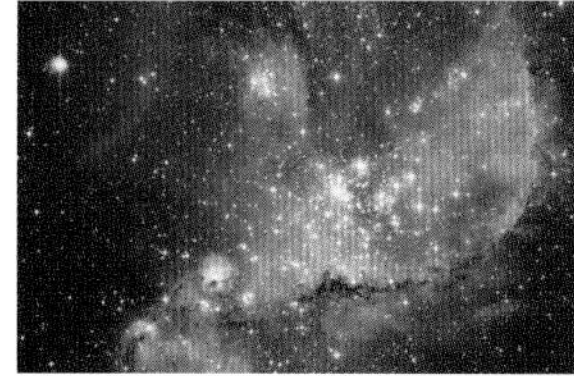

Light Year

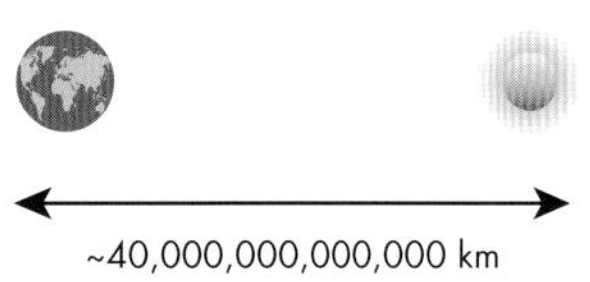

The amount of distance light can travel through space in one year. It is used to measure long distances in space. A light year equals about 9.46 trillion (9.46×10^{12}) kilometers or 5.88 (5.88×10^{12}) trillion miles.

Example:
Our nearest star is 4.24 light years away, so it takes light from that star 4.24 years to reach the Earth.

Main Sequence Star

A star that follows a standard pattern through its life, beginning in a blue-white stage and progressing through to a red stage.

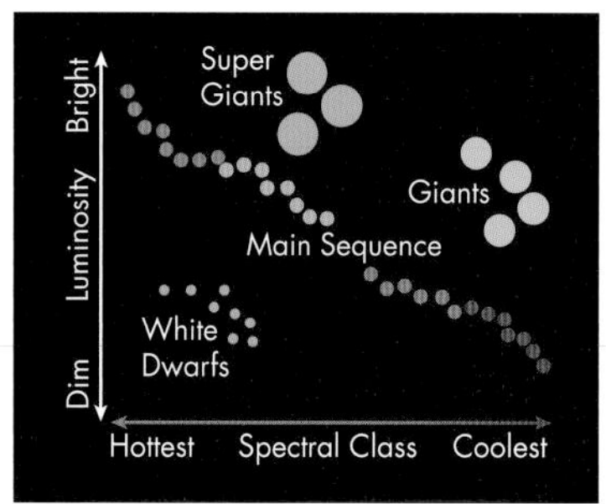

Meteor

A rock or piece of metal that burns as it enters the Earth's atmosphere. It may or may not make it to Earth's surface.

Meteorite

A rock or piece of metal that has fallen to Earth's surface from space.

Meteoroid

A rock or piece of metal in space. It may or may or may not enter the Earth's atmosphere.

Moon or Lunar Phases

The change in the appearance of the moon to an observer on Earth as the moon revolves around the Earth. See page 144 of the quick reference guide for a full lunar phase chart.

Nebula

A large cloud of space dust or gasses.

New Moon

New Moon

A phase of the moon in which the moon is between the sun and the Earth so the side facing the Earth does not receive any sunlight.

Orbit

The path an object follows when it goes around another object.

Example:
The outer planets orbit the sun.

Outer Planets

The giant gas planets in our solar system, farthest from the sun. They include Jupiter, Saturn, Uranus, and Neptune.

Prominence

An arc of flaming gas erupting from the sun's surface.

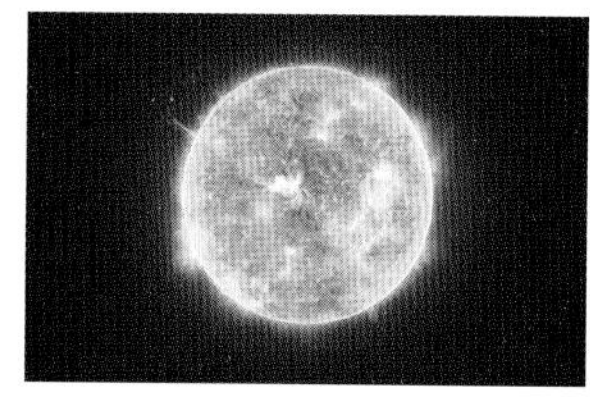

Protostar

A tightly packed cloud of material that is in the process of becoming a star.

Quarter

The phase of the moon in which half of the illuminated side of the moon is visible to Earth.

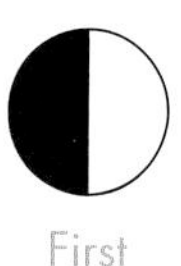
First Quarter

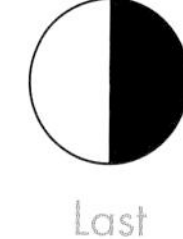
Last Quarter

Radio Telescope

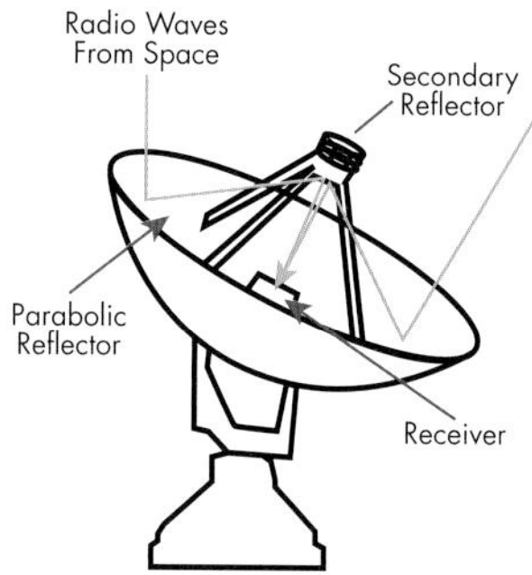

A telescope that collects radio waves given off by bodies in space. The radio waves then are translated into photographs based on the types of radio waves received. Scientists cannot look through radio telescopes.

Red Giant

A final stage in a star's life cycle in which it expands up to 500 times its original size as it cools down. See *Main Sequence Star*.

Reflecting Telescope

A telescope in which light from a faraway object is gathered, reflected, and focused by mirrors before being passed through the eyepiece to the observer.

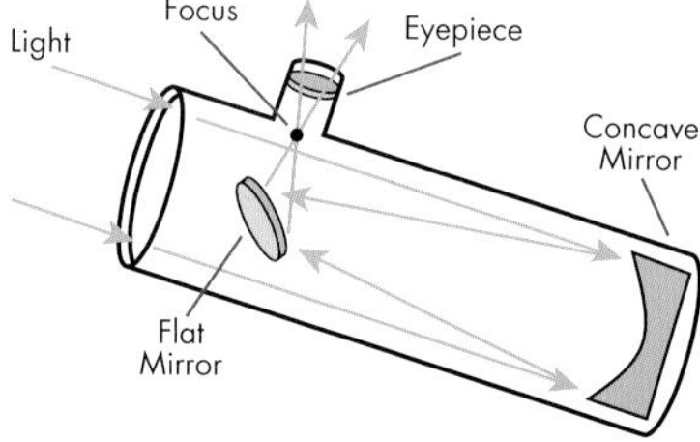

Refracting Telescope

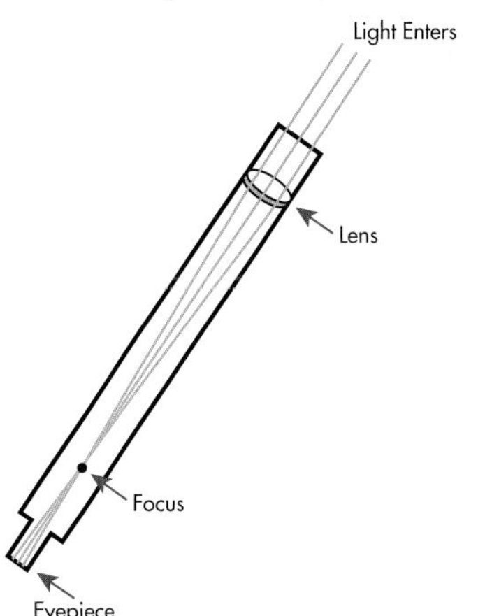

A telescope in which light from a faraway object is gathered and focused by various lenses before being magnified one more time as it passes through the eyepiece lens to the observer.

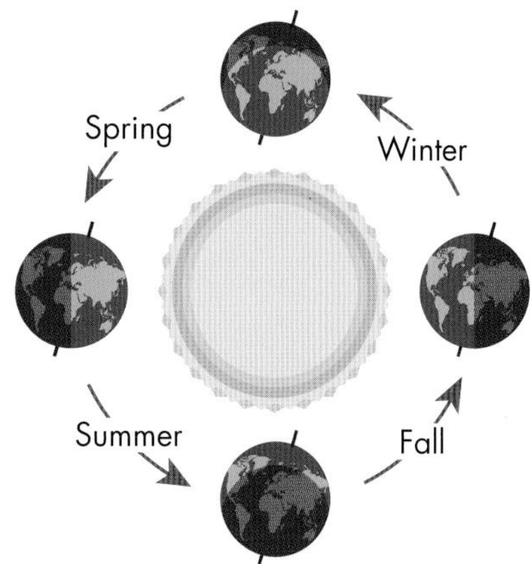

Revolution

The movement of a body around another in space. The Earth revolves around the sun, which accounts for our seasons. 1 orbit = 1 year.

Rotation

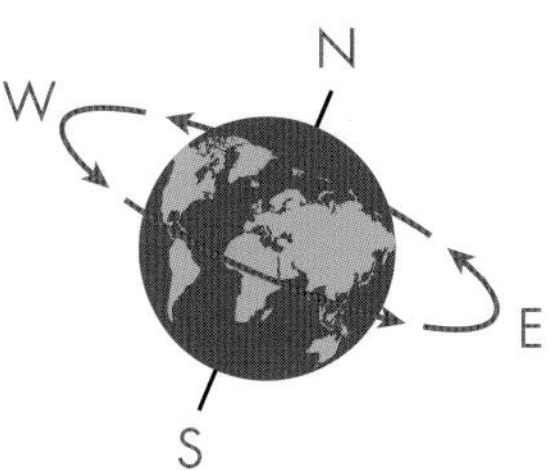

The turning on a center point or axis. The Earth's rotation on its axis causes day and night. 1 rotation = 1 day.

Satellite

A body in space that orbits a planet. It can be natural, like a moon, or manufactured.

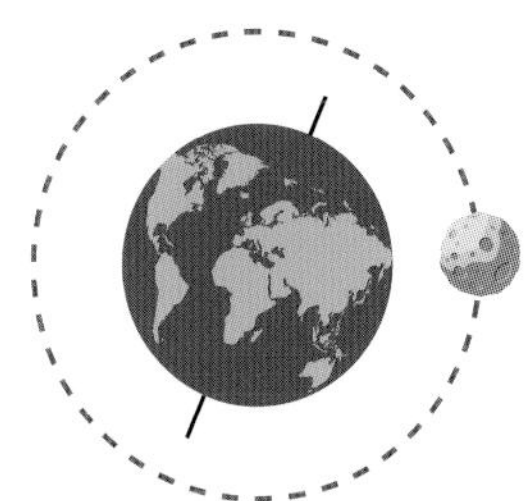

Solar Flare

A sudden eruption of hydrogen gas on the surface of the sun; appears as a very bright spot. It usually occurs near sunspots.

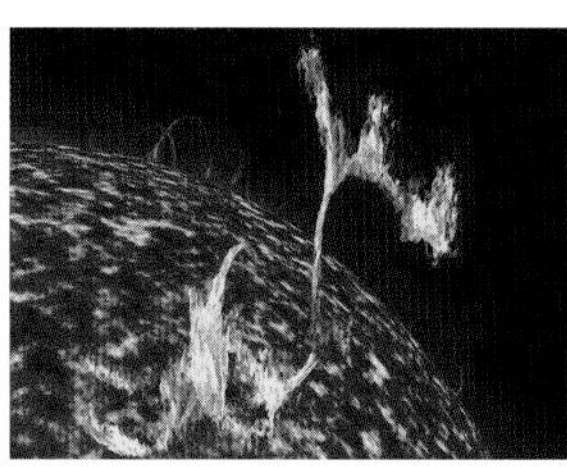

Space Probe

An unmanned (no people on board) spacecraft that is sent into space to send information back to Earth.

Examples:
Luna space probes that visited the moon, Mariner 9 that went to Mars, Mariner 10 that was sent to Mercury, and Voyager probes that send information back about the outer planets.

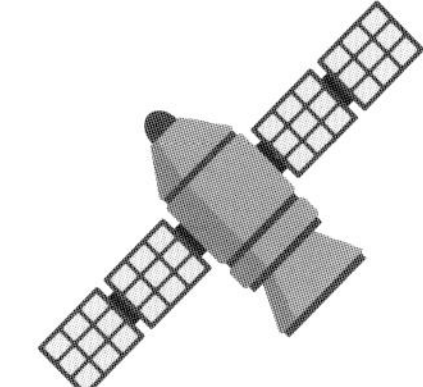

Spiral Galaxy

A galaxy that has arms that seem to "spiral" out from a compacted center. Made up of mostly young bright stars.

Examples:
Milky Way Galaxy, Pinwheel Galaxy

Sunspot

Cool, dark spots that appear on the sun's surface.

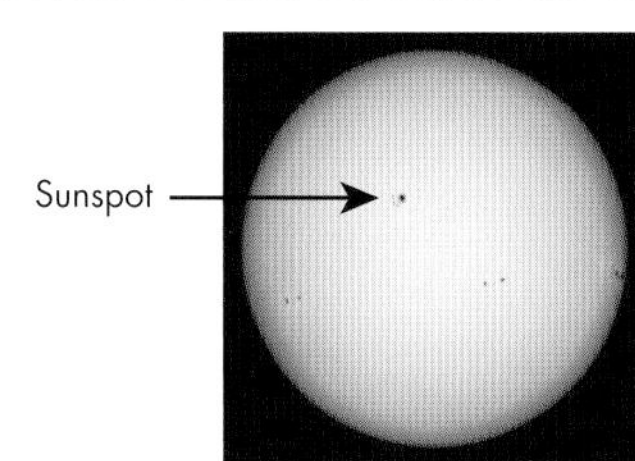

Supernova

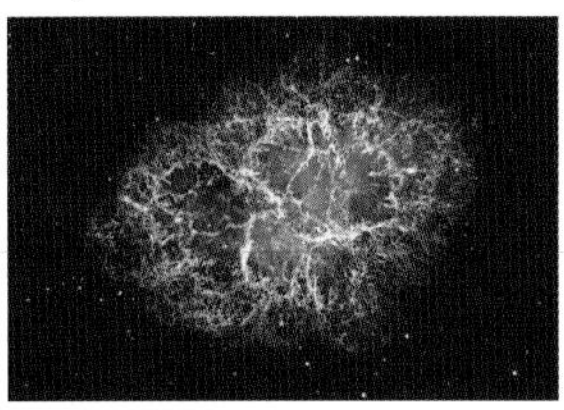

The explosion of a star that gives off lots of light and energy.

White Dwarf

The remains of a star after it has collapsed. Its particles are very tightly packed, and it does not give off much light. It is near the end of the cycle of a star. See *Main Sequence Star*.

Quick Reference Guides

USING LAB EQUIPMENT

Using a Microscope

1. Plug in the microscope and be sure the cord is tucked safely out of the way.
2. Move the objective lenses so the lowest power (the shortest lens) is pointing down toward the stage.
3. Place the slide on the microscope stage, putting it under the stage clips to keep it from moving. Be sure the specimen is over the middle of the hole in the stage. That will make it easier to find, but don't look yet!
4. Looking at the objective lenses, use the coarse focus (bigger knob) and move the lens to its lowest point, closest to the slide.
5. Look through the eyepiece and slowly turn the coarse focus until the specimen comes into focus.
6. Once it is in sight, if needed, adjust the fine focus to see more details.
7. If the specimen seems washed out or hard to see, adjust the diaphragm to allow less light to pass through the hole in the stage. This will bring out more detail.

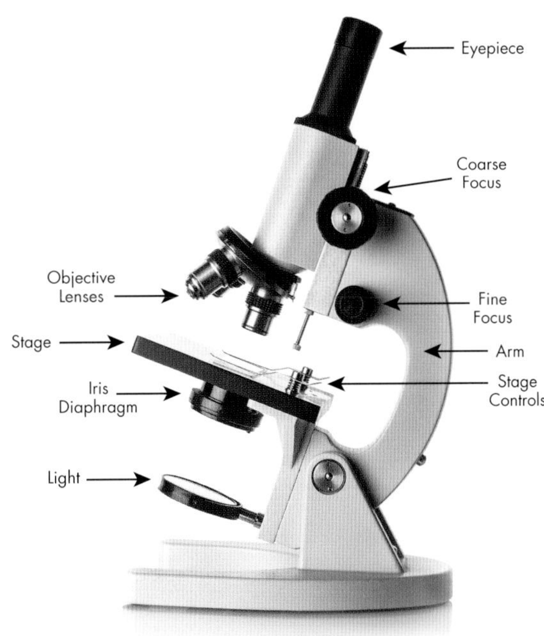

Using a Triple Beam Balance

1. Be sure the balance is zeroed, or measures zero, when there is nothing being massed. The balance indicator (usually a line on the right) should be lined up showing it's balanced. Different balances have different ways of zeroing them.
2. Place the object to be massed on the pan of the balance.
3. Starting with the largest (heaviest slider), move the slider into each notch along the beam until the balance indicator goes below the balance line.
4. Return the slider to the last notch it was in before it went too low.
5. Using the next smallest slider, move it from notch to notch until the balance indicator again goes below the balance line.
6. Return the slider to the last notch it was in.
7. Use the last slider (usually a small metal one without notches), and slide it slowly along the beam until the balance indicator and balance line match exactly.
8. Add the different numbers indicated on each beam to calculate the mass.

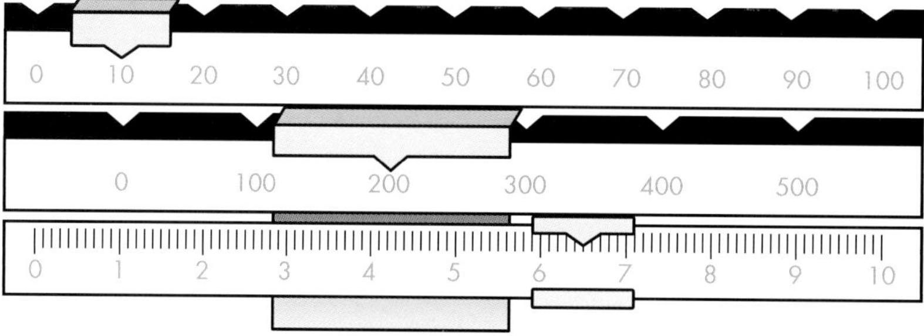

These beams read 10, 200, and 6.5, so the mass is 10 + 200 + 6.5, or 216.5 grams.

Using a Spring Scale

1. Be sure your scale is "tared," or measuring zero, when nothing is being weighed.
2. Attach the object to be weighed to the scale.
3. To measure the weight of the object, lift the object off the table using the scale.
4. To measure the force it takes to move an object, pull the object along the table or ground with the scale.

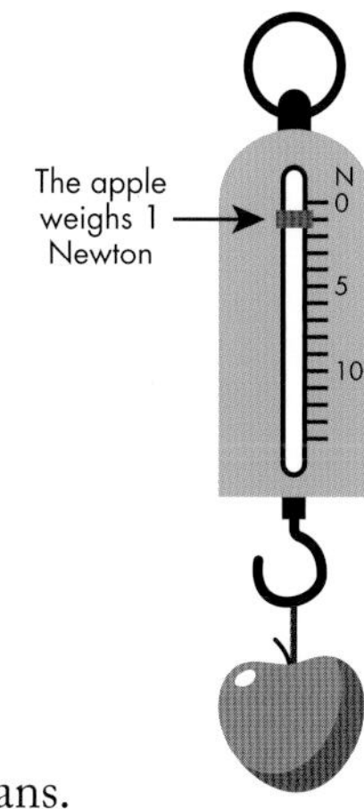

Using a Pan Balance

1. Place the objects you want to mass in one of the pans.
2. Place masses (or weights) in the other pan until the pans balance. There usually is a line or pointer that needs to be matched up to show exact balance.
3. Count the masses (or weights) that were put in the second pan to determine the mass of the object.

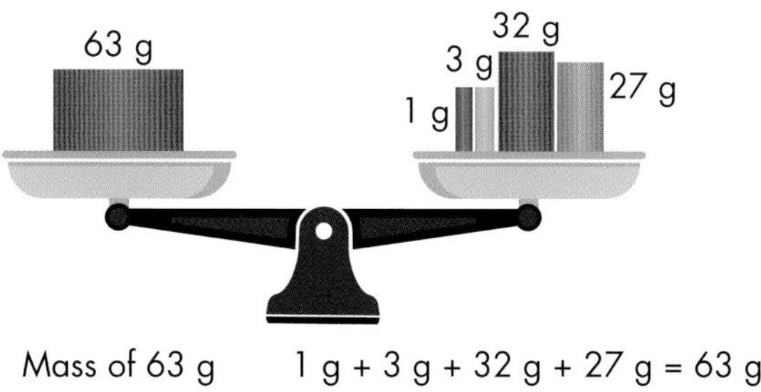

Mass of 63 g   1 g + 3 g + 32 g + 27 g = 63 g

Using an Eyedropper

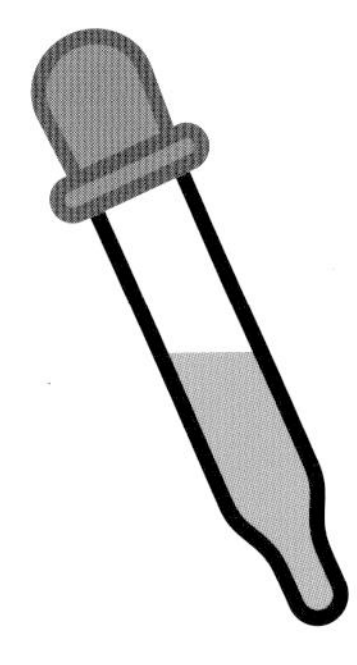

1. Squeeze the bulb at the top of the eyedropper.
2. Place the eyedropper into the liquid you want to transport.
3. Slowly release the bulb at the top to draw liquid into the eyedropper.
4. Without tipping or turning the eyedropper upside down, move it to the new location and slowly squeeze the bulb at the top to release the liquid one drop at a time.

Reading a Graduated Cylinder

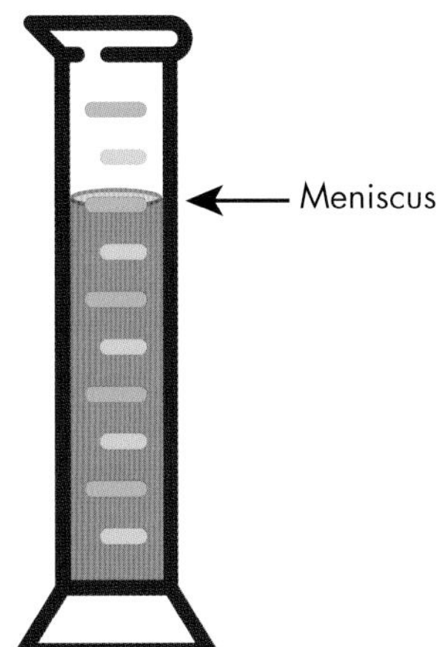

1. Be sure the graduated cylinder is on a flat surface.
2. Look at the curved level of the liquid in the cylinder. The curved surface is called a meniscus.
3. The lowest point of the meniscus is the volume of the liquid.

Note: Plastic graduated cylinders do not create meniscuses.

Measuring Volume

Measuring the volume of a regular solid:

1. Measure the length, width, and height of the object using a meter stick or ruler.
2. Multiply the measurements to get the volume.

Measuring the volume of an irregular solid:

1. Fill a graduated cylinder with water to a certain level.
2. Read the meniscus and record the volume of the water.
3. Add the solid to the graduated cylinder.
4. Record the new volume after the solid was added.
5. Subtract the two volumes to calculate the volume of the solid.

Measuring Volume, continued

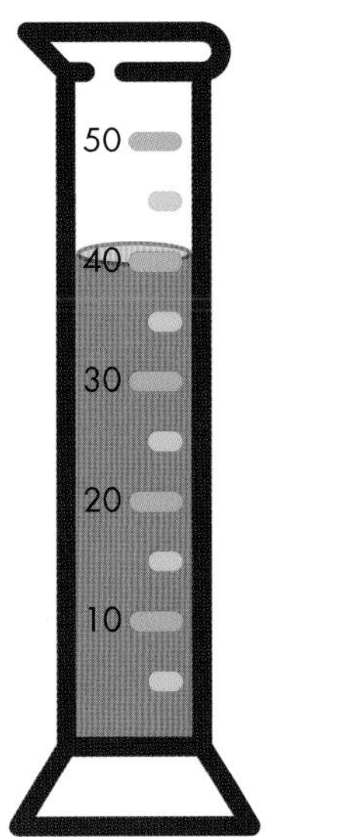

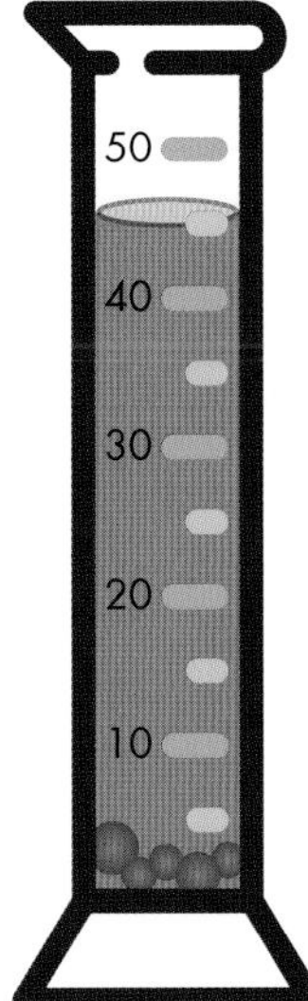

The initial volume in this cylinder was 40 ml. After the solid was added, it went up to 45 ml. The change was 5 ml, so that is the volume of the solid.

Calculating the Density of an Object

1. Find the mass of the object using a balance.
2. Find the volume of the object, either through measurement and calculation or through displacement using a graduated cylinder.
3. Divide the mass by the volume.

Example:
According to a triple beam balance, a rock has a mass of 56 grams. After putting it in a graduated cylinder and using displacement, the volume is 10 ml. The density is 5.6 g/ml or 56 grams/10 ml.

THE SCIENTIFIC METHOD

Steps of the Scientific Method

1. Identify the problem.
    a. Decide on a testable question that can be answered through experimentation.

2. Conduct research.
    a. Collect background information on the problem and the topic being studied.
    b. Find out what others already know about the topic and problem.

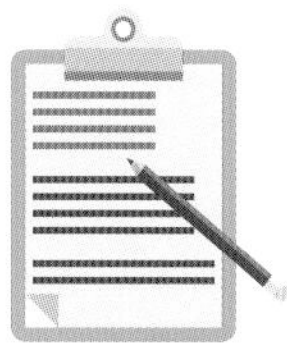

3. Create a hypothesis.
    a. Propose a solution to the problem based on the research and previous knowledge.

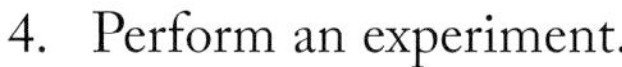

4. Perform an experiment.
    a. Test your hypothesis and collect the data.

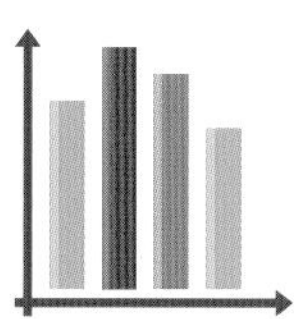

5. Analyze the data.
    a. Organize, examine, and graph the data obtained through the experiment.

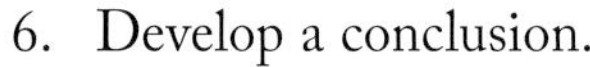

6. Develop a conclusion.
    a. Summarize the results of the experiment and its impact on the hypothesis.

Developing an Appropriate or Testable Question

The problem being investigated has a question that needs to be answered. This question needs to be testable in order to gather information and approach your problem.

To be sure your question or problem is testable, ask yourself these questions:

1. Can it be answered through an experiment?
2. Can you make observations in order to answer the question?

Developing an Appropriate or Testable Question, continued

3. Does it compare two things that can be measured?
4. Can you obtain quantitative data (using measurements) to answer this question?
5. Does it ask about objects, organisms, or events in the natural world?

Nontestable Questions

1. Depend on personal preference or moral values.
2. Ask about the supernatural.
3. Relate to ideas that cannot be measured.

Testable Questions	Nontestable Questions
Do vegetarians experience more heart attacks than meat eaters?	Is vegetarianism better than eating meat?
What if I added one more battery to a parallel circuit?	What is inside a battery?
How does temperature affect evaporation?	How do the seasons affect dogs?
How does soil type affect plant growth?	Which soil type is better?
What features of a parachute affect the time it takes to fall?	How does building height affect a parachute?

Tips for Writing Specific Procedures

1. Include a materials list with everything needed to complete the experiment.
2. Write the procedures step-by-step; do not leave anything out!
3. Number each step.
4. Make steps short, to the point, and easy to understand.
5. Include specific measurements as well as exact names of the equipment (e.g., 250 ml beaker rather than large cup).
6. Include a drawing or sketch to show how the experiment is set up if it will help.
7. Include any safety rules or cautions.
8. If possible, have another person read through your procedures to see if anything was left out.

COMMON LAB SAFETY RULES

1. Follow all written and verbal instructions carefully.
2. Do not work in the lab without a teacher present.
3. Wear safety goggles when instructed. Keep them on during the entire experiment, even if you or your lab group is already finished.
4. Conduct yourself in a responsible way at all times.
5. Only perform the experiment given or approved by your teacher.
6. Do not touch, smell, or taste any chemicals unless your teacher tells you to do so.
7. Always carry microscopes, triple beam balances, and glassware with chemicals using two hands.
8. Report an accident (breakage, spill, etc.) or injury to the teacher immediately.
9. Do not pick up broken glass or clean up any chemical spills.
10. Know where all of the safety equipment is located and how to use it.
11. Be sure the cords on any equipment are safely stored where they cannot be pulled or tripped over.
12. Never leave an open flame or hot plate unattended and never assume a hot plate is not hot.
13. Do not eat food, drink beverages, or chew gum.
14. Keep your hands away from your face, eyes, and mouth while using lab materials. Always wash your hands after an experiment.
15. Do not use or play with any equipment, supplies, or other materials in the science room without permission from the teacher.
16. Tie long hair back when working with equipment.
17. Treat any preserved biological specimens with respect.
18. Keep your work area neat and clean and clean all work areas and equipment at the end of the experiment.
19. Always dispose of any waste materials as instructed. Do not return unused chemicals to their original containers.

COLLECTING AND RECORDING DATA

Creating a Data Table

1. Identify the independent and dependent variables.
2. Decide on a title for your data table that tells the purpose of the data table.
3. Write your independent variable (what you are going to change and how) in the first column. Don't forget your units!
4. Make columns to record all of the details about your dependent variable (or results).
5. If appropriate, make more than one column for the dependent variable so more than one trial can be recorded.
6. If using more than one trial, include a column to calculate the average of the results.

Title

Independent Variable	Dependent Variable			Average of the Trials
	Trial 1	Trial 2	Trial 3	

The Effect of Ramp Height on Car's Travel Time

Height of Ramp (cm)	Time of Car on Track (sec)			Average of the Trials
	Trial 1	Trial 2	Trial 3	
5 cm	6.4 sec	6.2 sec	6.9 sec	6.5 sec
10 cm	5.2 sec	5.0 sec	4.8 sec	5.0 sec
15 cm	3.2 sec	3.5 sec	3.3 sec	3.3 sec

GRAPHING DATA

Creating a Bar Graph From a Data Table

The Effect of Ramp Height on Car's Travel Time

Height of Ramp (cm)	Time of Car on Track (sec)			Average of the Trials
	Trial 1	Trial 2	Trial 3	
5 cm	6.4 sec	6.2 sec	6.9 sec	6.5 sec
10 cm	5.2 sec	5.0 sec	4.8 sec	5.0 sec
15 cm	3.2 sec	3.5 sec	3.3 sec	3.3 sec

1. Identify the independent (what was changed in the experiment) and dependent (measured results of the change) variables.

   Independent = height of the ramp (centimeters)
   Dependent = time of car on track (seconds)

2. Label each axis with its variable. Be sure to include units if they are needed.

   Independent variable on the horizontal (x) axis
   Dependent variable on the vertical (y) axis

3. Determine the range of the data for each variable by subtracting the largest number from the smallest number needed on each axis.

   Height of ramp (x axis) = 15 cm – 0 cm = 15
   Time of car (y axis) = 6.5 sec – 0 sec = 6.5

4. Count the number of lines on each axis of your graph.

   15 lines on each axis

5. Divide the range for the y axis by the number of lines on your graph. This is will give you the value for each line on the y axis.

   Time of car on track (y axis) = 6.5 sec/15 lines = .43 sec/line
   (round to .5 sec/line)

Creating a Bar Graph From a Data Table, continued

6. Count the number of independent variables in the experiment to determine the number of bars.

   Heights: 5, 10, and 15, so 3 bars.

7. Decide how to place the bars (equally spaced) on the x axis.
8. Number the lines of your graph.
9. Use the data to create bars that show your quantities.

   (5, 6.5) (10, 5.0) (15, 3.3)

10. Give the graph a meaningful title.

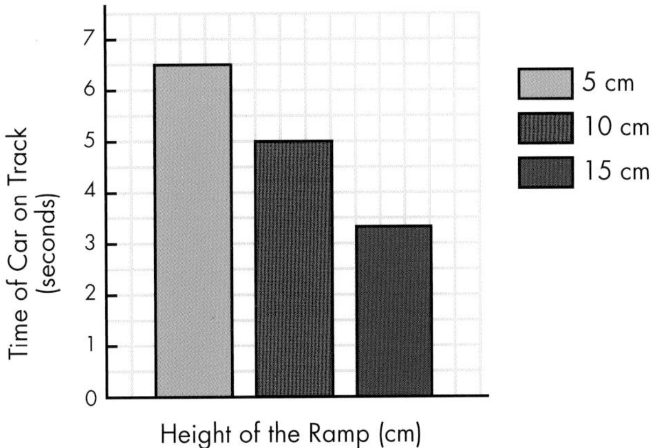

Creating a Line Graph Using Data From a Data Table

The Effect of a Heat Lamp on the Evaporation of Water

Number of Days Passed	Amount of Water Left (ml)			Average of the Trials
	Trial 1	Trial 2	Trial 3	
0	90 ml	90 ml	90 ml	90 ml
1	71 ml	72 ml	67 ml	70 ml
2	58 ml	58 ml	52 ml	56 ml
3	42 ml	46 ml	38 ml	42 ml
4	23 ml	27 ml	19 ml	23 ml
5	6 ml	8 ml	4 ml	6 ml

1. Identify the independent (what was changed in the experiment) and dependent (measured results of the change) variables.

   Independent = number of days passed
   Dependent = amount of water left (ml)

2. Label each axis with its variable. Be sure to include units if they are needed.

   Independent variable on the horizontal (x) axis
   Dependent variable on the vertical (y) axis

3. Determine the range of the data for each variable by subtracting the largest number from the smallest number needed on each axis.

   Number of days (x axis) = 5 days – 0 days = 5
   Amount of water left (y axis) = 90 ml – 0 ml = 90

4. Count the number of lines on each axis of your graph.

   15 lines on each axis

Creating a Line Graph Using Data From a Data Table, continued

5. Divide the range for each axis by the number of lines on your graph. This will give you the value for each line. Round your answers if you need to make it easier to plot your information.

   Amount of water left (y axis) = 90 ml/15 lines = 6 ml/line
   Number of days (x axis) = 5 days/15 lines = .33 days/line (use three lines for 1 day)

6. Number the lines of your graph.
7. Plot the data on your graph and connect the points.

   (0, 90) (1, 70) (2, 56) (3, 42) (4, 23) (5, 6)

8. Give the graph a meaningful title.

The Effect of a Heat Lamp on the Evaporation of Water

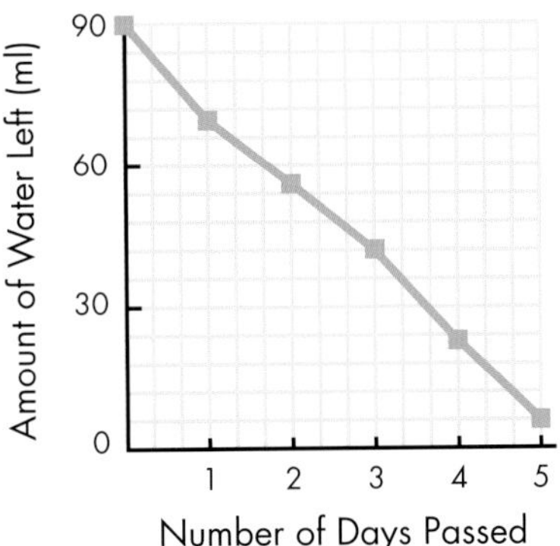

Creating a Multiple Line Graph

Number of Days Passed	Amount of Water Left		
	Under a Heat Lamp	Dark Closet	On the Classroom Table
0	15 ml	15 ml	15 ml
1	6.4 ml	15 ml	10 ml
2	0 ml	13.5 ml	6 ml
3	0 ml	12 ml	3 ml
4	0 ml	11 ml	0 ml
5	0 ml	9 ml	0 ml

1. Identify the independent (what was changed in the experiment) and dependent (measured results of the change) variables.

   Independent = time (days)
   Dependent = amount of water left (ml)

2. Label each axis with its variable. Be sure to include units if they are needed.

   Independent variable on the horizontal (x) axis.
   Dependent variable on the vertical (y) axis.

3. Determine the range of the data for each variable by subtracting the largest number from the smallest number needed on each axis.

   Number of days (x axis) = 5 days – 0 days = 5
   Amount of water left (y axis) = 15 ml – 0 ml = 15

4. Count the number of lines on each axis of your graph.

   15 lines on each axis

5. Divide the range for each axis by the number of lines on your graph. (This will give you the value for each line.) Round your answers if you need to make it easier to plot your information.

   Amount of water left (y axis) = 15 ml/15 lines = 1 ml/line
   Number of days (x axis) = 5 days/15 lines = .33 sec/line

Creating a Multiple Line Graph, continued

6. Number the lines of your graph.
7. Make a key for each of the sets of information that will be put on the graph and place it near your graph.

   Heat Lamp
   Dark Closet
   Classroom Table

8. Plot the data on your graph for each line and connect the points using the key to show each line.

   Heat lamp = (0, 15) (1, 6.4) (2, 0) (3, 0) (4, 0) (5, 0)
   Dark closet = (0, 15) (1, 15) (2, 13.5) (3, 12) (4, 11) (5, 9)
   Classroom table = (0, 15) (1, 10) (2, 6) (3, 3) (4, 0) (5, 0)

9. Give the graph a meaningful title.

The Evaporation Rate in Different Spots in Our School

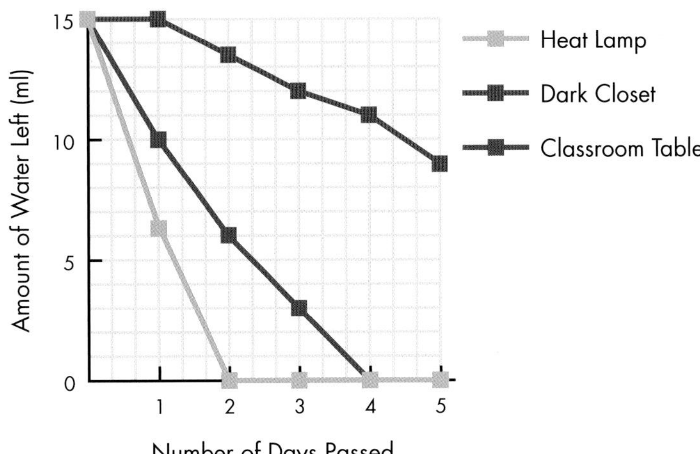

ATOMS

Calculating the Number of Protons

The number of protons is equal to the atomic number of the element.

Fluorine's atomic number is 9 = 9 protons

Calculating the Number of Neutrons

The number of neutrons is equal to the atomic mass minus the atomic number.

Fluorine has a mass of 18.9 (round to 19) – 9 (atomic number) = 10 neutrons

Calculating the Number of Electrons

In a stable atom, the number of electrons is equal to the number of protons, which is equal to the atomic number.

Fluorine has 9 protons = 9 electrons

Creating a Basic Bohr Model for an Element With an Atomic Number Between 1–20

1. Calculate the number of protons, neutrons, and electrons in the atom.
2. Place the protons and neutrons in the nucleus of your model.
3. After calculating the number of electrons, place them in their electron rings.

1st Ring = 2 electrons
2nd Ring = 8 electrons
3rd Ring = 8 electrons
4th Ring = 4 electrons

Determining if an Atom Is an Ion or an Isotope

1. Calculate the number of protons, neutrons, and electrons based on the periodic table.

Example:
Fluorine has 9 protons, 10 neutrons, and 9 electrons.

Determining if an Atom Is an Ion or an Isotope, continued

2. Compare the number of each particle in your question atom with the numbers you just calculated.

3. If the number of neutrons are different, it is an **isotope**.

Example:
Fluorine with 9 protons, 9 neutrons, and 9 electrons is an isotope. The number of neutrons is different from the one calculated based on the periodic table.

4. If the number of electrons is different, it is an **ion**.

Example:
Fluorine with 9 protons, 10 neutrons, and 10 electrons is an ion. The number of electrons is different from the one calculated from the periodic table.

Determining the Charge of an Ion

1. Using the periodic table, calculate the number of electrons for the atom.

Example:
According to the periodic table, Calcium should have 20 electrons.

2. Compare the number of electrons in your atom with what was calculated.

Example:
Our Calcium ion has 18 electrons, which is two less than the periodic table calculation.

3. If there are fewer electrons that what is stated on the table, your ion is positive by the difference.

   Because Calcium has 18 electrons, which is two less than the table, it is a positive 2 or 2+ ion.

4. If there are more electrons than what is stated on the table, your ion is negative by the difference.

Example:
If a Chlorine atom had 18 electrons, which is one more than is calculated from the table, that means the ion is negative by one or a 1– ion.

GENETICS

Creating and Completing Punnett Squares

Punnett squares are used to predict the genetic outcome of the offspring that may be produced when two organisms are bred together or "crossed."

1. Carefully read the given information for the cross.

   Complete a cross between a homozygous (purebred) short pea plant and a heterozygous (hybrid) tall pea plant.

2. Determine which trait is dominant (will always show if present) and which is recessive (will only show if no dominant trait is present).

   In pea plants, tall is dominant over short.

3. Designate letters for the trait or genes in the cross.

   Capital letters represent dominant traits, and lowercase letters represent recessive traits.
   T = tall plants
   t = short plants

4. Locate the important words in the cross to help you identify the makeup of each parent.

   homozygous or purebred = the plant has two of the same alleles (or letters) for this trait; so either TT (dominant) or tt (recessive)
   heterozygous or hybrid = the plant has different alleles for this trait; Tt

5. Using the information given, write the genotype (genes) for each parent.

   homozygous (purebred) short = tt
   heterozygous (hybrid) tall = Tt
   So: tt x Tt (Read as tt crossed with Tt)

6. List the genes that each parent can contribute to the cross.

   tt will contribute a t and a t
   Tt can contribute a T and a t

Creating and Completing Punnett Squares, continued

7. Draw a Punnett square and write the possible contributions from one parent along the top, and the other along the side.

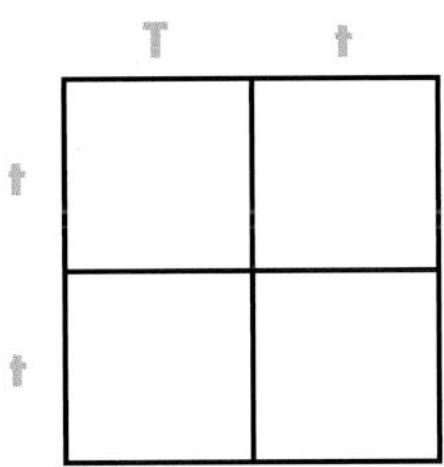

8. Fill in each box by writing the trait that is both above and beside it.

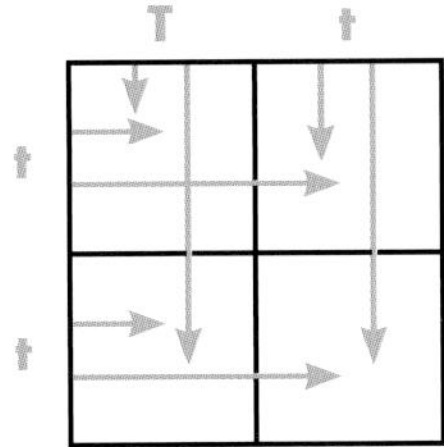

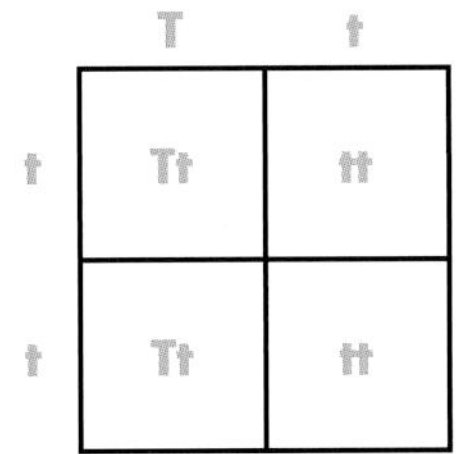

Determining the Genotypic Ratio From a Punnett Square

1. Complete your Punnett Square. The letters inside the square represent the genotype or genetic makeup of the offspring.

   Tt and tt in the example below.

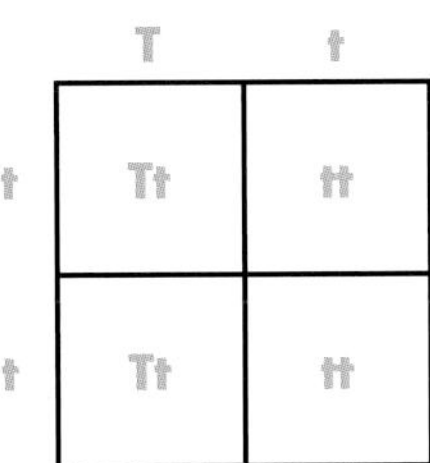

2. Count the number of each genotype.

   Tt = 2
   tt = 2

Determining the Genotypic Ratio From a Punnett Square, continued

3. Write down and reduce the ratio of each genotype produced in the cross.

   Tt to tt
   2 to 2 or reduces to 1:1.
   So its genotypic ratio is 1:1. For every plant that has genotype of Tt, there should be one with tt as its genotype.

Determining the Phenotypic Ratio From a Punnett Square

1. After completing your Punnett Square, write the phenotype of physical appearance of each offspring in its square.

	T	t
t	Tt tall	tt short
t	Tt tall	tt short

   Remember: Because a capital letter is the dominant trait, if there is at least one capital letter, the offspring will have that trait.

2. Count the number of each phenotype.

   Tall plants = 2
   short plants = 2

3. Write down and reduce the ratio of each genotype produced in the cross.

   Tt to tt
   2 to 2 or 1:1. Therefore, its phenotypic ratio is 1:1. For every short plant, there should be one tall one!

4. *Note*: The genotypic and phenotypic ratios are **not always** the same!

SOLUBILITY CURVES

Reading a Solubility Graph

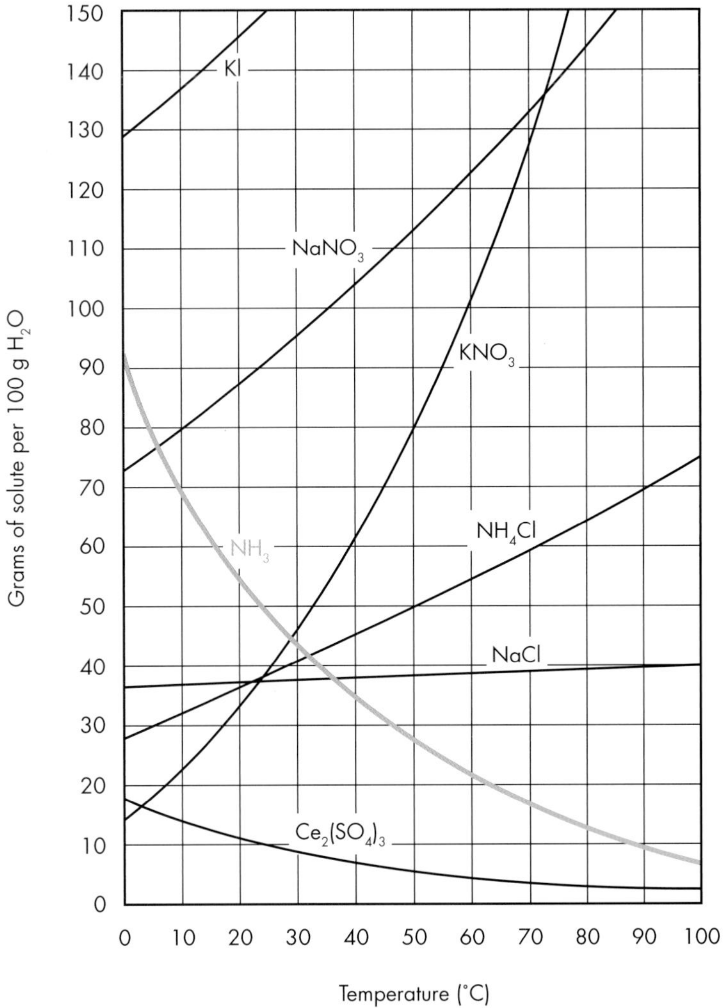

1. Locate the curve for the substance being dissolved. Ignore all of the other curves!

Let's use the NH_3 curve.

Reading a Solubility Graph, continued

2. To create a saturated solution, the curve will show the exact number of grams of the substance that can be dissolved in 100 grams of water at any temperature 0 °C–100 °C.

   For example, look at the curve and find 10 °C for NH_3. The curve shows 70 grams of NH_3 will create a saturated solution in 100 grams of water.

Determining the Solubility of a Solution

1. Locate the correct curve for the substance being dissolved.
2. Find the intersection of the amount of substance and the temperature of the water.
3. If the intersection of the two is below the curve for the substance, it is considered an unsaturated solution.

   For the temperature 10 °C, if there is 50 grams of NH_3 dissolved in the 100 grams of water, the solution is unsaturated.

4. If the intersection of the two is above the curve for the substance, it is considered a supersaturated solution.

   For the same temperature, if there are 90 grams of NH_3 dissolved in the 100 grams of water, then the solution is supersaturated.

FORMULAS

Motion

	Formula	Definition of Terms
Speed	$S=\frac{d}{t}$	S = speed d – distance t = time
Acceleration	$A=\frac{V_f-V_i}{t}$	A = acceleration V_f = the final velocity V_i = the initial or starting velocity t = the time for the acceleration to take place
Momentum	p = mv	p = momentum (kg • m/sec) m = mass (kg) v = velocity (m/sec)

Density

	Formula	Definition of Terms
Density	$D=\frac{m}{v}$	D = density m = mass v = volume

Temperature

	Formula	Definition of Terms
Celsius	°C = (5/9)(°F – 32)	°C = degrees Celsius °F = degrees Fahrenheit
Fahrenheit	°F = (1.8 × °C) + 32	°F = degrees Fahrenheit °C = degrees Celsius

Current

	Formula	Definition of Terms
Current	$I = \frac{P}{V}$	I = current (amps) P = power (watts) V = voltage (volts)
Current	$I = \frac{V}{R}$	I = current (amps) V = voltage (volts) R = resistance (ohms Ω)
Voltage	$V = I \bullet R$	V = voltage (volts) I = current (amps) R = resistance (ohms Ω)
Resistance	$R = \frac{V}{I}$	R = resistance (ohms Ω) V = voltage (volts) I = current (amps)
Power	$P = V \bullet I$	P = power (watts) V = voltage (volts) I = current (amps)

Waves

	Formula	Definition of Terms
Frequency	$F = \frac{v}{\lambda}$	F = frequency (Hertz) v = speed (usually in m/sec) λ = wavelength (in meters)
Wavelength	$\lambda = \frac{v}{F}$	λ = wavelength (in meters) v = speed (usually in m/sec) F = frequency (Hertz)

Mechanical Advantage of Simple Machines

	Formula	Definition of Terms
Inclined Plane	Mechanical advantage = $\frac{\text{Length of ramp}}{\text{Height of ramp}}$	Distance$_{\text{force or effort}}$ = measure of the length from the force to the fulcrum. Distance$_{\text{load or resistance}}$ = measure of the length from the fulcrum to the load.
Lever	Mechanical advantage = $\frac{\text{Distance}_{\text{force or effort}}}{\text{Distance}_{\text{load or resistance}}}$	
Wheel and Axle	Mechanical advantage = $\frac{\text{Radius of wheel}}{\text{Radius of axle}}$	

Weight

	Formula	Definition of Terms
Weight	$W = m \bullet g_c$	W = weight (Newtons) m = mass (kilograms) $g_c = 9.8\ m/sec^2$ (acceleration due to gravity constant)

Work

	Formula	Definition of Terms
Work	$W = F \bullet d$	W = work (watts) F = force (N) d = distance (meters)
Power	$P = \frac{W}{t}$	P = power (watts) W = work (watts) t = time (seconds)

TABLES AND CHARTS

Quick Conversions

Distance			
Metric to Metric	Metric to Standard	Standard to Metric	Standard to Standard
1 kilometer = 1,000 meters	1 kilometer = 0.621 miles	1 mile = 1.6 kilometers	1 mile = 5,280 feet
1 meter = 0.001 kilometers	1 kilometer = 3,281 feet	1 mile = 1,609 meters	1 mile = 1,760 yards
1 meter = 100 centimeters	1 meter = 1.0936 yards	1 yard = 0.914 meters	1 yard = 3 feet
1 meter = 1,000 millimeters	1 meter = 3.281 feet	1 yard = 91.44 centimeters	1 foot = 12 inches
1 centimeter = 10 millimeters	1 meter = 39.37 inches	1 foot = 0.305 meters	
	1 centimeter = 0.394 inches	1 foot = 30.48 centimeters	
	1 millimeter = 0.039 inches	1 inch = 2.54 centimeters	
		1 inch = 25.4 millimeters	
Mass and Weight			
Metric to Metric	Metric to Standard	Standard to Metric	Standard to Standard
1 kilogram = 1,000 grams	1,000 kg = 1.1 tons	1 pound = 0.454 kg	1 pound = 16 ounces
1 gram = 0.001 kilograms	1 kilogram = 2.20 pounds	1 pound = 453.59 grams	
1 gram = 1,000 milligrams	1 gram = 0.035 ounces	1 ounce = 23.349 grams	

Quick Conversions, continued

Volume			
Metric to Metric	**Metric to Standard**	**Standard to Metric**	**Standard to Standard**
1 liter = 0.001 kiloliters 1 liter = 1,000 milliliters 1 milliliter = 1 cm^3	1 meter ^{3} = 35 ft^3 1 liter = 0.264 gallons 1 liter = 1.057 quarts 1 liter = 2.1 pints 1 milliliter = 0.061 in^3 1 milliliter = 0.03 ounces	1 gal = 3.784 liters 1 quart = 0.946 liters 1 pint = 0.473 liters 1 pint = 473.176 milliliters	1 gallon = 8 pints 1 gallon = 4 quarts 1 quart = 2 pints
Area			
Metric to Metric	**Metric to Standard**	**Standard to Metric**	**Standard to Standard**
1 km^2 = 1,000,000 $meters^2$ 1 meter ^{2} = 10,000 $centimeters^2$ 1 cm^2 = 100 $millimeters^2$	1 km^2 = 0.4 $miles^2$ 1 meter ^{2} = 1.2 $yards^2$ 1 cm^2 = 0.16 $inches^2$	1 $mile^2$ = 2.6 km^2 1 $yard^2$ = 0.8 meter ^{2} 1 $foot^2$ = 929.03 cm^2 1 $inch^2$ = 6.451 cm^2	1 $mile^2$ = 640 acres 1 $yard^2$ = 9 $feet^2$ 1 $foot^2$ = 144 $inches^2$

Measurements and Their Units

Measurement	Unit Name	Symbol
Current	Ampere	A
Energy	Joule	J
Force	Newton	N
Frequency	Hertz	Hz
Power	Watt	W
Pressure	Pascal	Pa
Resistance	Ohm	Ω
Voltage	Volt	V
Weight	Newton	N
Work	Joule	J
Heat	Joule	J

Measurement	Common Units
Acceleration	m/sec^2, mi/hr/sec
Density	g/cm^3, g/ml
Distance	mm, cm, m, km
Mass	g, kg
Speed	m/sec, km/hr
Temperature	°C, °F, °K
Time	sec, hr
Volume	ml, l, cm^3
Distance in Space	AU

Metric Prefixes

Prefix	Symbol	Multiplier
giga-	G	1,000,000,000
mega-	M	1,000,000
kilo-	k	1,000
hecto-	h	100
deca-	da	10
deci-	d	0.1
centi-	c	0.01
milli-	m	0.001
micro-	μ	0.000001
nano-	n	0.000000001

Celsius and Fahrenheit

Celsius	Fahrenheit	Celsius	Fahrenheit	Celsius	Fahrenheit
0	32.0	34	93.2	68	154.4
1	33.8	35	95.0	69	156.2
2	35.6	36	96.8	70	158.0
3	37.4	37	98.6	71	159.8
4	39.2	38	100.4	72	161.6
5	41.0	39	102.2	73	163.4
6	42.8	40	104.0	74	165.2
7	44.6	41	105.8	75	167.0
8	46.4	42	107.6	76	168.8
9	48.2	43	109.4	77	170.6
10	50.0	44	111.2	78	172.4
11	51.8	45	113.0	79	174.2
12	53.6	46	114.8	80	176.0
13	55.4	47	116.6	81	177.8
14	57.2	48	118.4	82	179.6
15	59.0	49	120.2	83	181.4
16	60.8	50	122.0	84	183.2
17	62.6	51	123.8	85	185.0
18	64.4	52	125.6	86	186.8
19	66.2	53	127.4	87	188.6
20	68.0	54	129.2	88	190.4
21	69.8	55	131.0	89	192.2
22	71.6	56	132.8	90	194.0
23	73.4	57	134.6	91	195.8
24	75.2	58	136.4	92	197.6
25	77.0	59	138.2	93	199.4
26	78.8	60	140.0	94	201.2
27	80.6	61	141.8	95	203.0
28	82.4	62	143.6	96	204.8
29	84.2	63	145.4	97	206.6
30	86.0	64	147.2	98	208.4
31	87.8	65	149.0	99	210.2
32	89.6	66	150.8	100	212.0
33	91.4	67	152.6		

Common Household Acids and Bases

Substance	pH	Classification
Hydrochloric Acid (HCl)	0	acid
Battery Acid (H_2SO_4; Sulfuric Acid)	1.0	acid
Lemon Juice	2.0	acid
Vinegar	2.2	acid
Apple	3.0	acid
Soda Pop	4.0	acid
Tomato	4.5	acid
Coffee	5.0	acid
Milk	6.6	acid
Pure Water	7.0	neutral
Salt Water	7.0	neutral
Human Blood	7.4	base
Baking Soda (Sodium Bicarbonate)	8.3	base
Most Laundry Detergents	10.0	base
Milk of Magnesia	10.5	base
Ammonia	11.0	base
Lime (Calcium Hydroxide)	12.4	base
Lye	13.0	base
Drain Cleaner (NaOH)	14.0	base

Common Household Chemicals

Common Name	Chemical Name	Common Name	Chemical Name
ammonia	ammonium hydroxide	limewater	solution of calcium hydroxide
antacids	calcium carbonate	lite salt	potassium chloride
antifreeze	ethylene glycol	lye or soda lye	sodium hydroxide
asbestos	magnesium silicate	marble	mainly calcium carbonate
aspirin	acetylsalicylic acid	mercury oxide, black	mercurous oxide
baking soda	sodium bicarbonate	methanol	methyl alcohol
battery acid	sulfuric acid	milk of lime	calcium hydroxide
bicarbonate of soda	sodium hydrogen carbonate or sodium bicarbonate	milk of magnesium	magnesium hydroxide
black lead	graphite (carbon)	milk of sulfur	precipitated sulfur
bleaching powder	chlorinated lime; calcium hypochlorite	muriatic acid	hydrochloric acid
borax	sodium borate; sodium tetraborate	nail polish remover	acetone
brine	aqueous sodium chloride solution	plaster of Paris	calcium sulfate
chalk	calcium carbonate	Prussic acid	hydrogen cyanide
corn starch	amylose	quartz sand	silicon dioxide
cream of tartar	potassium bitartrate	quicksilver	mercury
dextrose	glucose	rock salt	sodium chloride
diamond	carbon crystal	rubbing alcohol	isopropyl alcohol
dry ice	carbon dioxide	soda water	carbonic acid
Epsom salts	magnesium sulfate	table salt	sodium chloride
glycerin	glycerol	table sugar	sucrose
gypsum	natural calcium sulfate	talc or talcum	magnesium silicate
household bleach	sodium hypochlorite	vinegar	impure diluted acetic acid
laughing gas	nitrous oxide	vitamin C	ascorbic acid
lime	calcium oxide	washing soda	sodium carbonate

Periodic Table

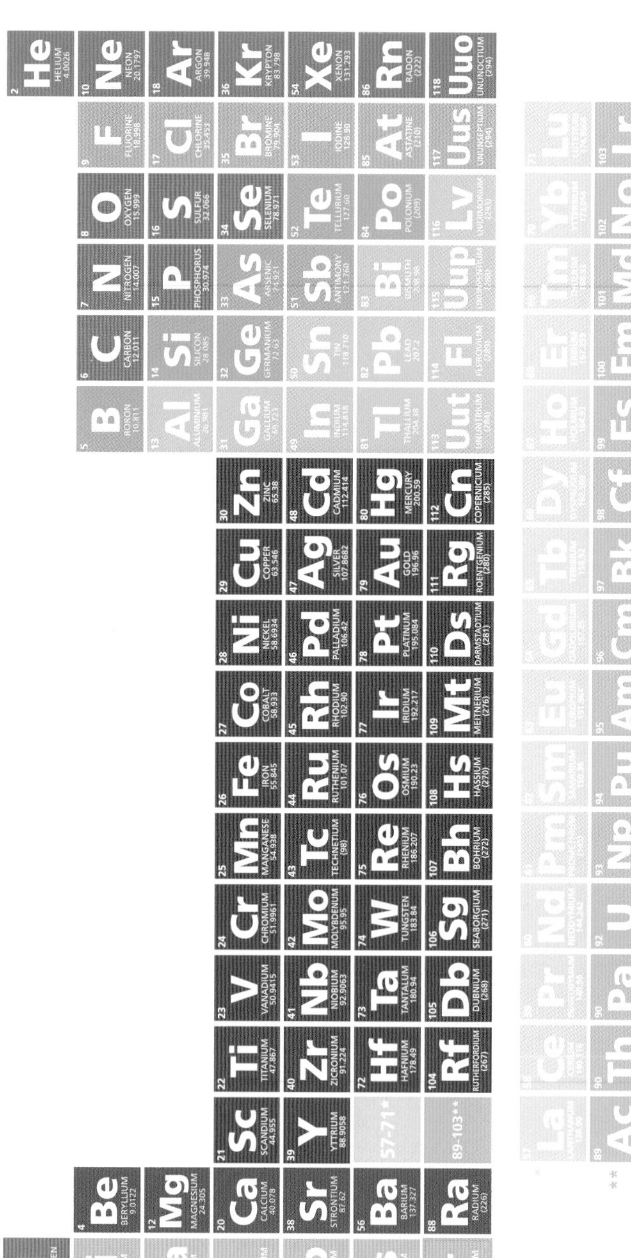

Noble Gasses
Halogens
Nonmetals
Metalloids
Other Metals
Transition Metals
Alkaline Earth Metals
Alkali Metals
* Lanthanides
** Actinides
Rare Earth Metals

Basic Weather Map Symbols

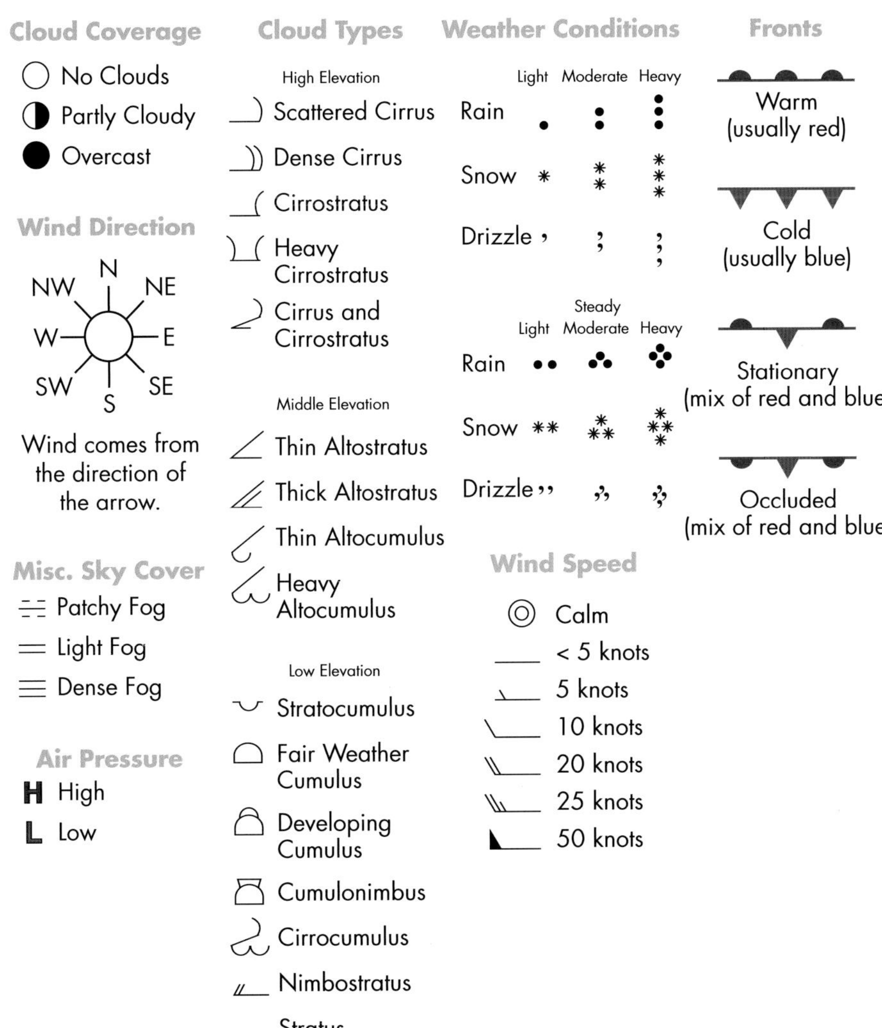
Cloud Coverage
No Clouds
Partly Cloudy
Overcast
Wind Direction
N
NW
NE
W
E
SW
SE
S
Wind comes from the direction of the arrow.
Misc. Sky Cover
Patchy Fog
Light Fog
Dense Fog
Air Pressure
H High
L Low
Cloud Types
High Elevation
Scattered Cirrus
Dense Cirrus
Cirrostratus
Heavy Cirrostratus
Cirrus and Cirrostratus
Middle Elevation
Thin Altostratus
Thick Altostratus
Thin Altocumulus
Heavy Altocumulus
Low Elevation
Stratocumulus
Fair Weather Cumulus
Developing Cumulus
Cumulonimbus
Cirrocumulus
Nimbostratus
Stratus
Weather Conditions
Light
Moderate
Heavy
Rain
Snow
Drizzle
Steady
Light
Moderate
Heavy
Rain
Snow
Drizzle
Wind Speed
Calm
< 5 knots
5 knots
10 knots
20 knots
25 knots
50 knots
Fronts
Warm (usually red)
Cold (usually blue)
Stationary (mix of red and blue)
Occluded (mix of red and blue)

Lunar Phases

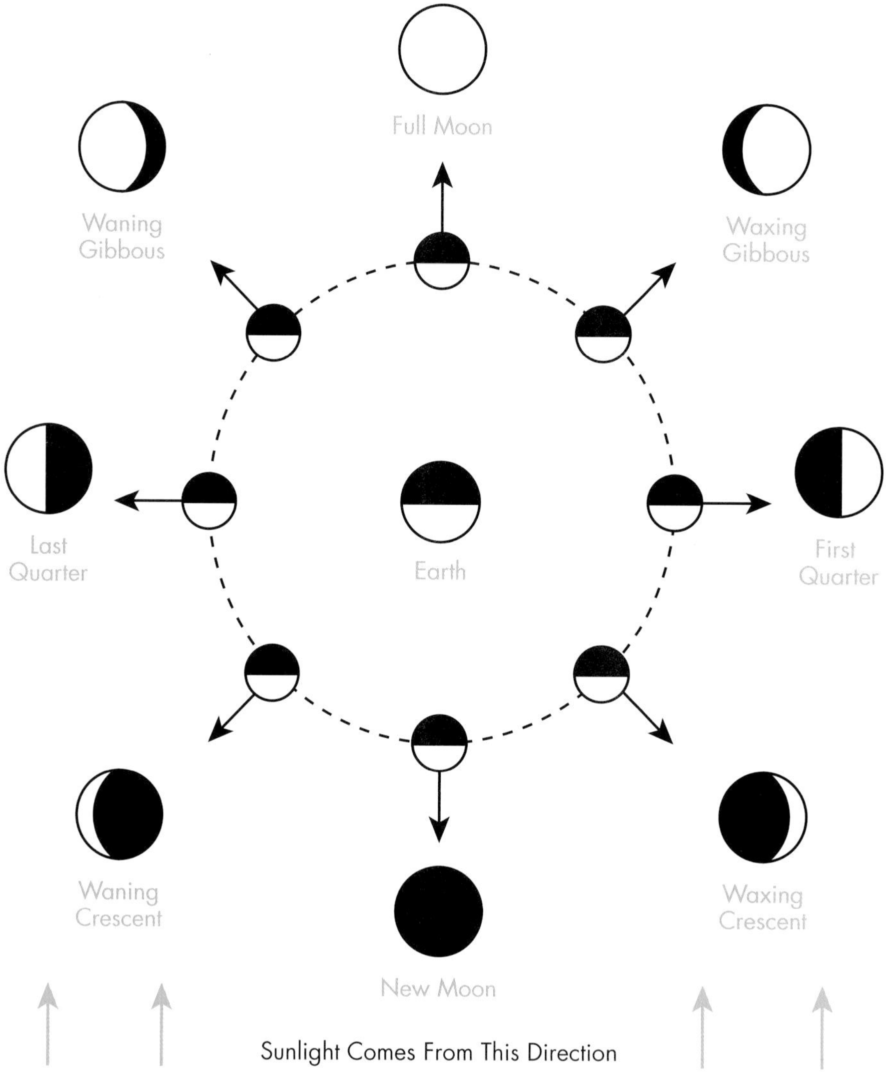

Full Moon

Waning Gibbous

Waxing Gibbous

Last Quarter

Earth

First Quarter

Waning Crescent

Waxing Crescent

New Moon

Sunlight Comes From This Direction

Moh's Hardness Scale

Hardness	Mineral	Description
1	Talc	Fingernail scratches it easily.
2	Gypsum	Fingernail scratches it.
3	Calcite	Copper penny scratches it.
4	Fluorite	Steel nail scratches it easily.
5	Apatite	Steel nail scratches it.
6	Feldspar	Steel nail does not scratch it easily, but the mineral scratches glass.
7	Quartz	Hardest common mineral. It scratches a steel nail and glass easily.
8	Topaz	Harder than any common mineral.
9	Corundum	It scratches topaz.
10	Diamond	Scratches all other minerals.

Geologic Timeline

Era	Period	Million Years Ago	Characteristic Life
Cenozoic	Quaternary	1.8	Birth of modern plants, animals, and man. Humans existed during the last 5–8 million years. Ice ages begin and end.
	Tertiary	65	"The Age of the Mammals": Modern whales and large mammals begin to appear, including horses, dogs, and bears.
Mesozoic	Cretaceous	146	"The Age of the Dinosaur": Extinction of reptile-like birds and many other reptiles by the end of this period. Dinosaurs are dwindling. Continents are located very much as they are now.
	Jurassic	208	First reptilian birds. Reptiles can be found in almost all habitats and biomes. Climate was warm all year round.
	Triassic	247	Pangaea broke apart. Earliest dinosaurs, flying reptiles, and marine reptiles existed. Primitive mammals appeared. Warm climate.

Geologic Timeline, continued

Era	Period	Million Years Ago	Characteristic Life
Paleozoic	Permian	280	"The Age of Amphibians": Primitive reptiles. Because of the change in climate from cold at the beginning to warm, a lot of species became extinct by the end. Pangaea exists.
	Pennsylvanian	330	Insects on the rise. Reptiles first appear. Climate warm and humid. The first cockroaches appear.
	Mississippian	360	Extinction of some fish species, while others diversified. Amphibians began to diversify. Plants die and begin to form present-day coal. First winged insects.
	Devonian	408	"The Age of the Fishes": Lots of fish, although many jawless varieties began to disappear.
	Silurian	438	Earliest known land animals. Primitive plants. Rise of fishes.
	Ordovician	505	Vertebrates appear with primitive plants. Trilobites and cephalopods abundant.
	Cambrian	540–500	"Age of the Trilobites": Lots of shallow seas. Earliest shellfish. Trilobites are common.
Precambrian	Proterozoic	2,500	Primitive plants and animals in the ocean. Changes in the Earth's crust produced major landmasses.
	Archeozoic or Archean	4,600	Formation of the Earth and slow development of the lithosphere, hydrosphere, and atmosphere. Development of sea life. Oldest known life (known through fossil records).

Note: From Geology.com (n.d.), Hyperphysics (n.d.)., & U.S. Geological Survey (2002).

References

Geology.com. (n.d.). *Geologic time scale*. https://geology.com/time.htm

Hyperphysics. (n.d.). *Geological time scale*. http://hyperphysics.phy-astr.gsu.edu/Hbase/Geophys/geotime.html

U.S. Geological Survey. (2006). *Geologic history of Southern California*. http://geomaps.wr.usgs.gov/socal/geology/geologic_history/index.html

INDEX

U

V

W

X

Z

About the Author

After teaching science for more than 15 years, both overseas and in the U.S., **Laurie E. Westphal, Ed.D.**, now works as an independent gifted education and science consultant nationwide. She enjoys developing and presenting staff development on low-stress differentiation strategies and using menus for various districts and conferences, working with teachers to assist them in planning and developing lessons to meet the needs of their advanced students. Laurie currently resides in Houston, TX, and has made it her goal to convert as many teachers as she can to the differentiated lifestyle in the classroom and to share her vision for real-world, product-based lessons that help all students become critical thinkers and effective problem solvers. She is the author of the Differentiating Instruction With Menus series as well as *Hands-On Physical Science*.